THE BIRTH OF A MIRACLE

God Still Works Wonders Today

DR. KIBBY OTOO

Published by Eden Creative Solutions
Lorton, Virginia
www.edencreativesolutions.com

ISBN 979-8-9986800-0-7 (paperback)

ISBN 979-8-9986800-1-4 (e-Book)

These ISBNs are the property of Eden Creative Solutions for the express purpose of sales and distribution of this title. The content of this book is the property of the copyright holder only. Eden Creative Solutions does not hold any ownership of the content of this book and is not liable in any way for the materials contained within. The views and opinions expressed in this book are the property of the Author/Copyright holder, and do not necessarily reflect those of Eden Creative Solutions.

Library of Congress Control Number: 2025907855

Printed in the United States of America.

To God, the Giver of every good and perfect gift. Through Him, miracles are not only possible but promised. This book is for His glory alone.

To my beloved wife, Elsie, and to my four daughters: Miracle, Christina, Zoe, and Angela. You are the living proof that God still performs wonders. Each of you is a testimony etched into our family story, a reminder that His Word never fails.

To my spiritual father, Archbishop Nicholas Duncan-Williams. Thank you for your prayers, your unwavering support, and for standing with us through every step of the journey. Your covering has been a shield and your faith an inspiration.

And to you, dear reader. It is my prayer that these pages become more than words. May they serve as a gateway, a spark that awakens your faith, opens your eyes, and ignites your expectation for the miraculous. May you move beyond merely reading about miracles to truly living them.

Contents

Preface

Every miracle has a story. It is never an accident, a coincidence, or a stroke of chance. A miracle is the visible eruption of the invisible God into human affairs—a divine interruption where impossibility bows to the authority of heaven.

Like natural birth, every miracle begins with conception. A word is spoken, faith is quickened, and hope takes root. It is carried in the hidden place of waiting, often tested by time, doubt, and warfare. Then comes the travail of prayer, obedience, and faith, until the moment of delivery arrives, when the unseen breaks forth into sight, and God's promise becomes your reality.

The pages ahead are not mere reflections but a prophetic journey. They are written to awaken faith, align your heart with God's order, and prepare you to conceive, carry, and manifest the miraculous in your own life.

This is more than a book: it is an altar. Come with expectation. Heaven is still in the business of birthing miracles.

Introduction

"For with God nothing will be impossible."
— Luke 1:3 7
(NKJV)

"Belief in miracles lies at the heart of authentic Christian faith."
— Walter Elwell

Miracles are not random occurrences of history. They are the fingerprints of God pressed onto the canvas of human impossibility. From the parting of the Red Sea to the raising of Lazarus, from Hannah's desperate prayer to Mary's virgin womb, Scripture reminds us again and again: God delights in doing what seems impossible.

But miracles are not just stories from long ago. They are not sacred accounts meant to be admired from a distance. The God who acted then is the same God who acts now. Jesus Christ, who opened blind eyes, multiplied loaves, and calmed raging storms, is "the same yesterday, today, and forever" (Hebrews 13:8). What

He did then, He is still willing and able to do today—in your life, your family, and your generation.

I believe this not only because the Bible says it, but because I have lived it. When my first daughter, Miracle, was born at just 24 weeks, she was so tiny and fragile that doctors doubted she would survive. By every medical measure, her story should have ended in sorrow. But God stepped in. He sustained her, healed her, and today she is a vibrant young woman, and the living proof that He still works wonders.

Her story did more than comfort my family; it also became a banner of hope for many others who were walking through valleys of fear and uncertainty. Friends, relatives, even strangers found strength through her testimony. And that is what miracles do. They don't stop with one person; they spread, igniting faith in others.

The journey of a miracle often follows a distinct rhythm:

- *The seed of promise:* God speaks, and faith awakens.
- *The womb of waiting:* Time stretches and tests, refining what we believe.
- *The labor of faith:* Prayer, trust, and obedience carry us through the struggle.
- *The delivery of manifestation:* When the unseen breaks into view, and what once seemed impossible becomes reality.

We see this pattern throughout Scripture. Abraham and Sarah embraced Isaac after years of waiting. Hannah poured out her heart in prayer and was given Samuel. Mary surrendered to God's Spirit and carried the Savior of the world. Each of these stories shows that when God speaks, His Word does not return empty. It conceives, it carries, and it brings forth life.

And so it can be with you. The miracle you are waiting for is not beyond reach. It is already alive in the heart of God, waiting for your faith to meet His power.

That's why I wrote this book. It is not only the record of my daughter's story, or even of my family's testimonies. It is meant to remind you that your story, too, can become a living testimony of God's power. Whether you are believing for healing, longing for a child, standing in the middle of uncertainty, or simply trusting God for a breakthrough, these pages are for you.

So, I invite you: read with expectation. Every Scripture is more than words; it is a doorway. Every testimony is more than encouragement; it is an invitation. Every prayer is more than ink on a page; it is a seed waiting to bear fruit.

Your miracle has a beginning.

Your testimony has a future.

And your life can become undeniable evidence that God still works wonders.

Welcome to the birthplace of miracles.

Part One
Foundations of the Miraculous

Every great move of God begins with a foundation. Before we can fully understand, pursue, or sustain the miraculous, we must return to the bedrock truths of who God is and why He works in power. Without that foundation, miracles can be misunderstood, counterfeited, or even idolized. But when they are anchored in Scripture and in the heart of God, miracles become more than wonders. They become windows into His eternal purposes.

The miraculous is not a side theme in the Bible. It is a central thread woven through God's relationship with humanity. From creation itself, when God spoke light out of darkness, to the resurrection of Christ, which secured our redemption, miracles reveal a consistent truth: God is present and active in His world. They are not simply interruptions of the natural order; they are moments when divine order breaks into human chaos.

This foundation matters because it keeps us from chasing signs without knowing the God of the signs. It protects us from deception and reminds us that miracles flow out of God's nature, His covenant, and His unchanging love. As we explore the foundations of the miraculous together, we will see that miracles are not distant echoes of biblical history but timeless expressions of the God who still works wonders today.

1

The God Who Works Miracles

"You are the God who performs miracles; you display your power among the peoples."

— Psalm 77:14

From the opening pages of Genesis to the closing vision of Revelation, the Bible reveals a God who is not distant or passive, but deeply involved with His creation. He is not only able to perform miracles; He is Himself the Miracle-Worker. His very nature is to do what human effort and natural law could never achieve. He is the God who steps into impossibility with the power of eternity.

Throughout Scripture, His miracles reveal who He is, how He works, and why the miraculous remains essential for understanding His relationship with humanity.

God the Miracle-Worker in Creation

The Bible begins with the greatest miracle of all: creation itself. *"In the beginning God created the heavens and the earth"* (Genesis 1:1). God had no raw materials, no blueprints, and no assistance. Yet when He spoke, the universe came into being.

Out of nothing, He called forth galaxies. Into formless chaos, He spoke order. Into darkness, He declared light. Into emptiness, He released abundance. Every star, every mountain, every ocean, every living creature exists because the Miracle-Worker opened His mouth and said, *"Let there be ... "*

Creation is not just an ancient event. It is a lasting testimony of God's nature. The God who began with impossibility is the same God who sustains His people through impossibility.

Genesis alone gives us glimpses of His power in different ways:

- *The miracle of life:* God formed Adam from the dust and breathed His own Spirit into him (Genesis 2:7). Humanity began not by accident but by divine intention—a miracle that marks every soul with eternal worth, not just for this life but for eternity.
- *The miracle of a child of promise:* Sarah, barren in old age, conceived Isaac by the promise of God (Genesis 21:2). Her story reminds us that God's promises are not limited by biology or human limitation.
- *The miracle of God's plan:* Joseph, betrayed and imprisoned, was lifted to Egypt's throne (Genesis 41).

Through him, God showed that even the hardest seasons can become part of His greater purpose. He turns setbacks into platforms and betrayal into breakthrough.

From the very beginning, God reveals Himself as the One who makes the impossible possible. Genesis is not just the story of beginnings. It is the unveiling of the Miracle-Worker's nature, a God who creates, redeems, and raises His people above the limits of the natural order.

And if the God who spoke galaxies into existence also formed you, knows you, and breathes life into you, then no impossibility in your life is beyond His reach. The same hands that set the stars in place hold your future. The same voice that said *"Let there be light"* still speaks into darkness today.

God the Miracle-Worker in Covenant

When humanity fell, God's wonders did not end. They multiplied, this time as acts of redemption. From the beginning, miracles were tied to God's promises—expressions of His faithfulness even when His people were unfaithful.

In the Exodus, He shattered Egypt's gods with signs and wonders. Plagues struck the land until Pharaoh released God's people. The Red Sea parted, giving Israel dry ground to walk on, then closed over their enemies (Exodus 14).

In the wilderness, God revealed Himself not only as Deliverer but also as Provider and Sustainer. Water flowed from a rock, manna rained from heaven, quail filled the camp (Exodus 16–17). Their clothes and shoes did not wear out, nor did their strength fail (Deuteronomy 29:5). Each miracle declared the covenant promise: *"I will never leave you nor forsake you."*

The covenant power of God continued throughout Israel's journey. Jordan's floodwaters parted as Joshua led Israel into their inheritance, the Promised Land (Joshua 3). The walls of Jericho fell at the sound of trumpets and a shout of faith (Joshua 6). Gideon's three hundred men defeated an army far larger than themselves, armed only with torches, trumpets, and God's presence (Judges 7).

Through the prophets, God's covenant love shone again. Fire fell from heaven at Elijah's prayer on Mount Carmel, consuming sacrifice, water and stone alike (1 Kings 18). Oil multiplied for a widow, the dead were raised, and Naaman was healed of leprosy through Elisha's ministry (2 Kings 4–5). Every miracle was more than a supernatural wonder. They all carried a message: *"I am with you. My promises remain. I have not abandoned you."*

And every covenant miracle pointed forward to the greatest covenant of all—the New Covenant, when God Himself came in flesh and sealed His promises at the cross with His own blood.

God the Miracle-Worker in the Prophets

The prophets walked as living witnesses of God's power. They were more than people who predicted the future. They were carriers of His presence. Their lives were living messages that Yahweh is the only true God, faithful to His promises and mighty to save.

Elijah, known as the prophet of fire, stood on Mount Carmel before a nation torn between two opinions and called down fire from heaven. The flames consumed the sacrifice, the stones, the water, and even the dust, proving that Baal was powerless and that Yahweh alone is God (1 Kings 18:36–39). Later, Elijah prayed, and rain returned after years of drought. His life proclaimed a miracle-working God who both judges and restores.

Elisha, who succeeded Elijah, carried a double portion of that prophetic anointing. Through him, God multiplied a widow's oil until it filled every vessel, raised the Shunammite woman's son from death, purified a poisoned stew, and cleansed Naaman, the Syrian commander, from leprosy (2 Kings 4:1–7, 2 Kings 4:32–41; 2 Kings 5:1–14). To this day, the name Elisha is remembered for stories of miraculous provision, healing, and resurrection.

Other prophets also bore witness to God's power. Isaiah foretold that a virgin would give birth to a Son (Isaiah 7:14), pointing to Christ. Daniel was preserved in the lions' den, while his three friends walked unharmed through fire (Daniel 3:16–27; 6:16–23). Jonah, swallowed by a great fish and delivered after three days, became both a sign of God's mercy and a foreshadow of Christ's resurrection (Jonah 1:17; Matthew 12:40).

Through these prophets, God's power was revealed not only to Israel but also to the nations. Each miracle was both a divine interruption and a declaration that no empire, idol, or circumstance could stand against the covenant-keeping God of Israel.

Yet, each prophetic miracle pointed beyond itself, to the One who would come as the Prophet greater than Moses, greater than Elijah, greater than all: Jesus Christ, the Miracle-Worker in whom every prophetic promise would find its "Yes and Amen."

God the Miracle-Worker in Christ

The fullness of God's miracle-working power is revealed in Jesus. He is the Word made flesh (John 1:14), the image of the invisible God (Colossians 1:15), the radiance of His glory

(Hebrews 1:3). In Him, miracles were not distant events but the living expression of God's heart walking among men. Every healing, deliverance, and sign revealed not only the power of God but His compassion, justice, and covenant love.

Jesus Himself explained, *"The Son can do nothing by Himself; He can only do what He sees His Father doing"* (John 5:19). Every miracle of Christ was the Father's will displayed on earth.

The miracles Jesus touched every part of life:

- *Nature:* He turned water into wine, calmed storms, and walked on the sea (John 2:1–11; Mark 4:39; Matthew 14:25).

- *Sickness:* He healed lepers, opened blind eyes, unstopped deaf ears, and made the lame walk (Luke 17:11–19; John 9:1–7; Mark 7:31–37; John 5:1–9).

- *Death:* He raised Jairus' daughter, the widow's son at Nain and Lazarus after four days in the tomb (Mark 5:41–42; Luke 7:14–15; John 11:43–44).

- *Need:* He multiplied bread and fish to feed multitudes, demonstrating that He is the Bread of Life (Matthew 14:13–21; 15:32–39).

- *The demonic:* He cast out unclean spirits with authority, breaking the chains of torment and proving that the kingdom of God had come near (Mark 1:25–26).

Yet the greatest miracle of all was His death and resurrection. On the cross, He bore the sin of the world. In the grave, He broke the power of death. In His resurrection, He secured eternal victory for all who believe (1 Corinthians 15:55–57). Every other miracle pointed to this supreme act of redemption: the miracle of salvation itself.

And Jesus did not stop with His own works. He invited His

followers to continue them: *"Whoever believes in Me will also do the works I have been doing, and they will do even greater things than these"* (John 14:12). The miracles of Christ were never meant to end with Him, but to flow through His Body, the Church, until He returns.

God the Miracle-Worker in the Church

After Jesus ascended, the miracle-working power of God did not cease. Rather, it multiplied, as the Holy Spirit came upon the disciples with fire and power on the Day of Pentecost (Acts 2). The same Spirit who hovered over creation and raised Jesus from the dead now indwelt ordinary men and women, turning them into vessels of God's wonders.

Miracles in the Early Church were both the seal and the fuel of the Gospel's advance:

- At Pentecost, tongues of fire rested upon the disciples, and they spoke in languages unknown to them, declaring God's glory to the nations (Acts 2:1–12).
- At the Beautiful Gate, Peter and John lifted a lame man to his feet, and he leapt, walked, and praised God (Acts 3:6–8).
- Through the apostles, "many signs and wonders were regularly done among the people" (Acts 5:12).
- Through Philip's ministry, demons fled and the paralyzed were healed, bringing great joy to Samaria (Acts 8:5–8).
- Through the Apostle Paul, the sick were healed by handkerchiefs that touched his body, and even the dead were raised (Acts 19:11–12; Acts 20:9–12).

The miracles were not random displays of power; they were

kingdom proclamations. Each healing, deliverance, or sign testified that Jesus was alive, the Spirit had come, and the Father's kingdom was breaking into earth.

Paul affirmed this in Romans 15:18–19: *"By the power of signs and wonders, through the power of the Spirit of God... I have fully proclaimed the gospel of Christ."* Miracles were never entertainment but evidence of the Gospel.

Miracles were not limited to the apostles. Stephen performed wonders (Acts 6:8), Philip worked signs in Samaria, and the early believers prayed, *"Lord, stretch out Your hand to heal, and perform signs and wonders through the name of Your holy servant Jesus"* (Acts 4:30), and God answered.

The miracle-working God was present in His Church then, and He is with us still. The Spirit of God has not departed. The same Jesus who walked the shores of Galilee now walks among His lampstands (Revelation 1:13), empowering His people with signs that follow (Mark 16:17–18).

Miracles in the Church remind us that we are not merely an institution, but a living body animated by the Spirit of God. They declare that Jesus Christ is alive, and His power is available to all generations who believe.

God the Miracle-Worker in Revelation

The final book of the Bible does not end the story of miracles; it crowns it. Revelation unveils God's ultimate triumph great signs and wonders: seals broken, trumpets sounding, and bowls poured out in judgment and mercy. Nations tremble, kings bow, angels wield power beyond measure, and Satan is finally overthrown.

What John saw was not mere imagery, but the unfolding of God's power and promises to their final completion. Each one points to the final victory of Christ and the unshakable hope that belongs to His people.

Revelation shows us the ultimate miracles:

- The Lamb who was slain now reigns on the throne (Revelation 5:6–13).
- The dead are raised and judged (Revelation 20:12–13).
- Satan and death are cast into the lake of fire (Revelation 20:10, 14).
- Heaven and earth are made new as the New Jerusalem descends (Revelation 21:1–2).

The last promise is the greatest miracle of all: *"Behold, I make all things new"* (Revelation 21:5). The God who began history with *"Let there be light"* will bring it to completion with eternal glory, dwelling with His people forever: *"Behold, the dwelling place of God is with man. He will dwell with them, and they will be His people, and God Himself will be with them as their God. He will wipe away every tear from their eyes, and death shall be no more"* (Revelation 21:3–4).

The Unchanging Nature of the Miracle-Worker

Across all of Scripture, one truth resounds like a trumpet: God has not changed. He is still the Miracle-Worker. His character is constant, His covenant unbreakable, and His power unchallenged.

From creation to redemption to eternity, His wonders reveal His heart. What He did for His people then, He is doing still. For He Himself declares: *"I am the Lord, I do not change"* (Malachi 3:6). And Hebrews affirms: *"Jesus Christ is the same yesterday, today, and forever"* (Hebrews 13:8). What God did for Abraham, Elijah, Daniel, Mary, and Paul, He will do again—because His character does not change, His covenant does not fail, and His promises remain "Yes and Amen" in Christ (2 Corinthians 1:20).

Dear reader, this is your confidence: the same God who opened barren wombs, parted seas, healed lepers, fed multitudes, and raised the dead is alive, present and active in your life today. His love has not faded, His power has not weakened, and His promises have not failed.

So lift your faith. Tear down every ceiling of unbelief. Silence the whispers of impossibility. Remember: the Miracle-Worker has not retired, grown weary, or withdrawn His hand. Even now, He is moving, healing, restoring, and revealing His glory.

And the greatest miracle is still to come, when all creation is renewed, death is swallowed up in victory, every tear is wiped away, and the kingdom of God is revealed in fullness. Until then, every miracle you experience is a glimpse of the eternal power of the unchanging God who reigns forever.

Be assured. Be expectant. Be bold. The Miracle-Worker is with you, in you, and for you—and His wonders have only just begun.

THOUGHTS FOR REFLECTION

1. When you think of God as the Miracle-Worker, which biblical story speaks most to you right now, and why?
2. Of the examples from this chapter —Creation, Covenant, Prophets, Christ, the Church, or Revelation— which most strengthens your faith today?
3. Where in your life are you facing an "impossible" situation that needs God's intervention?
4. How does remembering that God never changes build your confidence to believe Him again?

5. What is one step you can take to position yourself to expect God's miraculous power?

PUT IT INTO PRACTICE

Choose one "impossible" situation in your life and write it down. Each time doubt arises, declare: *"The Miracle-Worker has not changed. What He did then, He can do again."* Let this declaration shape your expectation as you move forward.

2

The Language of Miracles

"Unlike the modern world, the ancient world was not suspicious of miracles. They were regarded as a normal, if somewhat extraordinary, part of life."

— Walter Elwell

Have you ever witnessed a miracle? I have. In fact, my very life began as one. I wasn't supposed to be here. My mother intended to abort me, but the procedure failed. My existence itself is evidence of God's intervention. Throughout my life, there have been many moments when I cannot explain how I survived, endured, or prevailed, except that it was the hand of

God guiding me. That's why the subject of miracles is so close to my heart.

But what exactly is a miracle? A miracle is a supernatural act, an intervention from God that goes beyond what the natural world can explain. It is when circumstances defy natural explanation and can only be attributed to a supernatural cause.

The Bible describes miracles as events that "run counter to the observed processes of nature."[1] C.S. Lewis called them "an interference with nature by supernatural power."[2] Simply put, miracles are moments when God steps into human history to reveal His power and His love in ways nature cannot explain.

But miracles are not just extraordinary events. They are a language, a divine conversation written across creation, history, and human experience. From Genesis to Revelation, God speaks through signs and wonders, revealing not only what He does but who He is. When we learn to read this language, we discover His presence, His compassion, and His purposes.

Important Truths About Miracles

The Bible does not present God as a distant deity who wound up the universe and stepped away. Instead, it reveals a Father who is deeply involved in the lives of His people. Miracles are the clearest demonstration of this reality— a language of signs and wonders that show us who He is.

1. **Miracles reveal God's love.** Every miracle carries the heartbeat of God's compassion. When Jesus touched the leper, it was love that moved Him to act (Mark 1:41). Each miracle is God's way of saying, *"I see you, I care for you, and I will help you."*

2. **Miracles reflect God's nature.** They are not random

displays of power but windows into His character. Feeding the five thousand revealed His generosity (Matthew 14:13–21). Calming the storm revealed His protective care (Mark 4:39). In every miracle, His kindness, mercy, and grace shine through.

3. **Miracles confirm God's faithfulness.** Again and again, God's promises were sealed by miraculous acts. Abraham and Sarah conceived Isaac in old age. Hannah bore Samuel after years of barrenness. These miracles declared that His Word never fails.

4. **Miracles renew faith and hope.** When the lame man was healed at the temple gate (Acts 3:6–10), his restored legs lifted more than just his body; they lifted the faith of everyone who saw him. Miracles have a ripple effect, stirring hope and expectancy not only in the one who receives but in all who witness them.

5. **Miracles display God's sovereignty and power.** When seas parted, walls collapsed, and the dead were raised, God was revealing His rule over creation, history, and even life itself (Psalm 135:6; Mark 4:39). They remind us that nothing is beyond His authority.

6. **Miracles point us back to God's glory.** They are never an end in themselves. Each one is a signpost directing us to worship the One who works them. At Pentecost, the wonders that filled the upper room prepared hearts for Peter's message, and thousands believed (Acts 2:41–43).

7. **Miracles foreshadow God's redemptive plan.** Every healing, every deliverance, every resurrection points forward to Christ. In Him, the greatest miracle was revealed: God Himself restoring creation and offering eternal life (Luke 7:22; John 11:25–26).

The Language of Miracles in Scripture

The Gospels use four main words to describe the supernatural works of Jesus[1]: wonders, signs, power, and works (Acts 2:22). Each reveals a different way God speaks through miracles—a language that shows His presence and purposes.

Wonders capture attention and awaken awe. They stir amazement and remind us that God is greater than the natural world. When Jesus calmed the storm with a word or raised Lazarus from the grave, people marveled because they saw something no human could accomplish. Wonders draw us into holy reverence.

Signs point to God's presence and authority. They reveal that every miracle is intentional. They are signs because they point beyond themselves. When Jesus healed the blind man (John 9), it was a sign of God's glory and Christ's authority. Signs communicate—God is speaking, and He wants us to listen.

Power demonstrates God's strength breaking into human reality. Every healing, deliverance, or breakthrough shows that God's power is still active and able to overturn the impossible.

Works describe the purposeful deeds that flow from Christ's mission. His miracles weren't just about meeting immediate needs. Feeding the five thousand revealed His care for people's needs. Casting out demons revealed His authority over darkness. Every work was intentional, pointing back to the Father's heart.

Together these four terms remind us that miracles are not only about results. They are God's way of speaking, with meaning and a message.

Different Kinds of Miracles

Miracles come in many forms. Some are spectacular, while others are so ordinary we might overlook them. Together, they reveal that God is always at work, both in the world around us and in our daily lives.

One kind is what we might call *natural miracles*. These are the wonders of creation we often take for granted or explain away with science. But explanation does not cancel wonder.

Creation itself is God's first language of signs and wonders. With a word, He spoke light into darkness (Genesis 1:3). From dust, He formed Adam and breathed life into him (Genesis 2:7). The earth's orbit, tilt, atmosphere, and perfectly timed seasons are not accidents but ongoing miracles of divine design. Even the invisible shield protecting us from harmful radiation testifies that God sustains life with precision. Creation reminds us that if He could form a universe from nothing, He can speak life into our emptiness today.

Another kind is *everyday miracles*. These are moments of divine grace woven into daily life that we often overlook. Life, breath, and waking each morning are gifts we easily take for granted. Yet every heartbeat is a miracle of God's sustaining grace. The fact that you and I exist—out of millions of possible genetic combinations—is nothing short of miraculous. Provision, protection, even timely guidance are daily mercies that carry His fingerprints. Every meal on the table, every close escape from danger, every recovery from sickness—whether gradual or sudden—reminds us that God is intricately involved in our lives. These small miracles tune our hearts to recognize His hand, preparing us to trust Him for greater things.

For this book, however, our focus will be on what most people think of when they hear the word "miracle": *supernatural miracles*, like those recorded in the Bible. These are the miracles that defy every natural explanation. Hebrews 11 recalls barren women conceiving, seas parting, walls collapsing, kingdoms overthrown, and lions' mouths shut. In the Gospels, the blind see, the lame walk, and the dead are raised.

These are the moments when heaven invades earth and impossibilities bow to God's power. These are the miracles we often long for most, the ones that break chains of impossibility.

Together, the natural, the everyday, and the supernatural declare one truth: God is always working. The ordinary trains our eyes to see Him in daily life, while the extraordinary reminds us that nothing is impossible with Him.

Why Don't We See More Supernatural Miracles?

This is an honest question many believers wrestle with: If God is the same yesterday, today, and forever, why do spectacular miracles seem rarer today?

OUR CULTURE TEACHES SKEPTICISM

We live in a world shaped by scientific thinking, where only what can be proven in a lab is accepted as real. Miracles, by definition, defy natural laws. They are supernatural. In modern culture, anything unexplainable is often dismissed or ridiculed.

Sadly, this mindset has seeped into the Church. Many believers, without realizing it, adopt a skeptical attitude. We might say God *can* do miracles, but quietly think of them as rare, unrealistic, or reserved for biblical times. Yet Scripture reminds us: God does not change (Malachi 3:6; Hebrews 13:8).

RELIGION WITHOUT RELATIONSHIP

Another reason miracles seem scarce is that faith is often reduced to rituals and routines. People may attend services, recite prayers, or follow rules, but without intimacy with God. Miracles thrive in an atmosphere of intimacy with God. When faith becomes just rules, routines, and services, it loses power.

Jesus rebuked this kind of worship: *"These people honor me with their lips, but their hearts are far from me"* (Matthew 15:8). A living relationship creates space for faith and dependence, the soil where the supernatural grows.

LOSS OF EXPECTANCY AND TEACHING

In many churches today, there is little anticipation for God to move. When teaching about and demonstration of the supernatural are absent, faith weakens, and believers stop asking God for big things. We begin to lower our expectations to match our experiences, instead of allowing the Bible to shape them.

But Jesus declared in Mark 9:23 (NLT): *"Everything is possible if a person believes."* Faith isn't about pretending we never doubt. It's about taking God at His word, even when we don't see results immediately.

SELECTIVE BELIEF IN GOD'S WORD

Some Christians accept only the "comfortable" parts of the Bible and downplay the parts that display the supernatural power of God. They prefer a "safe" faith that doesn't challenge them to believe for miracles.

Yet the Bible is full of the miraculous, from Genesis to Revelation. To cut out the supernatural is to cut out part of God's revelation of Himself. The Apostle Paul of a form of godliness that denies its power (2 Timothy 3:5). True faith embraces *all* of who God is, including His miraculous power.

DISAPPOINTMENT AND UNANSWERED PRAYER

For many, the absence of miracles comes with real pain. They prayed earnestly but didn't see the outcome they hoped for. This disappointment makes it hard to trust again. If that's you, God sees your hurt. Faith doesn't mean denying your pain. It means bringing it to God anyway, believing He is good even when you don't understand.

Some answers come differently than expected, and some come only in eternity (Isaiah 55:8–9). Yet Jesus invites us to keep asking, seeking, and knocking (Matthew 7:7–8).

NEGLECT OF THE HOLY SPIRIT

Many believers simply don't understand the Holy Spirit's role in the miraculous. Jesus Himself relied on the Spirit to preach, heal, and perform miracles (Luke 4:1; Acts 1:8). As believers, we can't experience the supernatural without the help of the Holy Spirit. Without relying on the Spirit, our faith becomes human effort alone, unable to produce supernatural results. The Holy Spirit is the channel through which God's power flows to us and through us.

The Spirit empowers us to pray according to God's will, hear God's voice, and walk in obedience even when it doesn't make sense. He gives spiritual gifts, builds faith, and creates the atmosphere where miracles can happen. Without Him, our faith is limited to what we can see and do on our own.

FEAR OF MAN AND REJECTION

Finally, some believers hold back from praying boldly or sharing their testimonies because they're afraid of being ridiculed or seen as fanatical. Yet Revelation 12:11 declares that we overcome by the blood of the Lamb and the word of our testimony. When we share what God has done in our lives, our faith strengthens and others are stirred to believe.

As we draw this chapter to a close, let's remember that miracles are more than events. They are God's living language. Every miracle you witness, experience, or declare is God speaking—inviting you into relationship, trust, and awe. power.

In this book, my desire is to help you reclaim expectancy. Throughout these pages, you will read testimonies of people who have seen God do the impossible in conception, childbirth, healing, and many other situations.

My prayer is that these stories will stir your faith and remind you that miracles are not just records from the past. They are God's way of reminding us that He is near, active, and faithful. Look for them, receive them, and proclaim them. The Miracle-Worker is still telling His story through the miraculous, and He desires to write a fresh chapter through your life.

THOUGHTS FOR REFLECTION

1. Am I treating faith as a ritual, or as a relationship?
2. Do I really expect God to move in my life today?
3. Am I willing to ask boldly, even when it feels risky?
4. Am I depending on the Holy Spirit, or on my own strength?
5. Am I willing to share my testimony to build others' faith?

PUT IT INTO PRACTICE

God still speaks, not only through written words but also through living expressions of His power. To "read" this language, we must posture our hearts to discern His voice in everyday life.

Here are four ways to cultivate this posture:

- *Listen*: Open your ears and spirit to His Word, for Scripture is His primary voice. Be attentive also to the Spirit's whispers, nudges, and inner stirrings. Even ordinary moments can carry extraordinary direction if you are paying attention.

- *Expect*: Approach each day with the confidence that God is still at work. Expectancy is the soil where miracles take root. When you carry an open heart, you live ready for His interruptions.

- *Respond*: When God prompts you, take action. Pray with boldness, and obey His instructions, even when they stretch your comfort. Faith without response remains dormant, but faith expressed becomes the channel of God's power.

- *Share*: Your testimony is never just your story; it is a declaration of God's faithfulness. Speaking it strengthens your own faith and plants seeds of expectation in others. Every testimony becomes an invitation for God to "do it again."

3

The Birthplace of Miracles

Miracles do not happen by chance. They are conceived in the divine meeting point of God's Word, His Spirit, and our faith. From Genesis to Revelation, we see a consistent pattern: God speaks His Word, the Spirit gives it life, faith holds it, prayer and obedience labor for it, and in time the miracle comes into view. Understanding this "birthplace" helps us partner with God for the impossible in our own lives.

The Word: The Seed of Promise

The very first miracle was creation itself. God spoke, and it came to be (Genesis 1:3). Light pierced the darkness. Land, stars, and life appeared at His command. From the beginning, the pattern is clear: every miracle starts with God's declaration.

The same is true in human history. God promised Abraham and Sarah a son, and the promise of Isaac was conceived long before they ever held him (Genesis 17:19; 21:2). Hannah prayed in faith, and Samuel was carried in her heart before he was born (1 Samuel 1). The widow of Zarephath obeyed Elijah's instruction, and her oil multiplied (1 Kings 17). Mary received the angel's message and yielded herself to God's plan, and the Savior of the world was born (Luke 1:38).

God's Word is always the seed. Faith takes root when we hear it, believe it, and welcome it into our hearts. Without His Word, there is no conception and miracles remain distant stories instead of present reality.

The Spirit: The Power to Bring Life

God's Word is the seed, but the Spirit is the breath that makes it live. Just as creation was formed by the Spirit hovering over the waters (Genesis 1:2), in the same way, the Spirit moves over the seed of promise in our hearts.

Jesus, full of the Spirit, began His ministry with power (Luke 4:1, 14). Every healing, deliverance, and sign came through the Spirit's presence. And before His ascension, He promised that same Spirit to His followers: *"But you will receive power when the Holy Spirit comes upon you"* (Acts 1:8).

The Spirit is the channel of God's supernatural power. Without Him, faith is reduced to human effort. With Him, the invisible begins to move toward the visible. He stirs expectation, aligns timing, and supplies the power for God's Word to manifest in our lives.

Faith: The Womb of Waiting

Faith is not wishful thinking. It is the living posture of trust, perseverance, and obedience. When the Word of God is planted and the Spirit breathes upon it, faith becomes the womb where miracles take shape.

Faith has always carried God's promises through seasons of waiting. Abraham and Sarah carried the promise of Isaac for decades, learning that delay is not denial. Hannah prayed through years of barrenness until Samuel was born. The disciples waited in Jerusalem until the Spirit came at Pentecost, turning waiting into wonder.

Waiting, then, is not wasted time. It is God's incubation period, where He strengthens belief, aligns hearts, and prepares circumstances for supernatural birth. In this womb of waiting, faith wrestles with doubt, persists through testing, and clings to God even when everything visible whispers "impossible."

Travail: Prayer and Obedience

If faith is the womb, then prayer and obedience are the labor pains that push the miracle into manifestation. God, in His sovereignty, could act alone; but again and again in Scripture we see that He chooses to involve His people. He invites us to partner with Him through prayer and faith-filled obedience. Miracles are not earned, but they often require a response.

The widow of Zarephath had to obey Elijah's instruction in order to see the miracle of supernatural provision. By pouring out her last oil, she positioned herself for God's abundance, and the jar did not run dry (1 Kings 17). Mary also had to yield when the angel announced God's plan. Her simple words, *"Let it be to me according to your word"* (Luke 1:38), opened the way for the Savior to be born. The disciples, too, pressed into prayer and fasting, and as they sought God together, boldness and guidance were released for the next stage of their mission (Acts 1–2).

Travail is rarely comfortable, but it is always purposeful.

Prayer refines our hearts and draws us into God's will. Obedience, even when costly, positions us for the fulfillment of His promise.

Understand this: the miracle is conceived in faith, but it is delivered through travail. When your faith refuses to quit, and your obedience yields to God's timing, what was once unseen will be birthed into reality.

Manifestation: When the Invisible Becomes Visible

At last, the promise breaks through. What once lived only as a word from God, carried in faith and prayed over in perseverance, steps into reality.

Isaac was born to Abraham and Sarah, proving that God's promises never expire. Samuel was dedicated by Hannah, showing that tears sown in prayer can become songs of joy. The widow's oil overflowed, revealing that God can take what little we have and make it more than enough. And at the fullness of time, Christ entered the world, the ultimate miracle, God in human flesh.

Every breakthrough follows this divine pattern: God speaks His Word, the Spirit breathes life, faith carries it, prayer and obedience labor for it, and in time the miracle is revealed. But manifestation is never only about the miracle itself. It is about the God it reveals. Every breakthrough whispers the same truth: His Word cannot fail, His Spirit still moves, and His power is available today.

Your Miracle Today

Your miracle is not beyond reach. It is already alive in the heart of God. The same Spirit who overshadowed Mary is still at work in you. Every prayer you offer in alignment with God's Word and will becomes labor toward birth. Every step of obedience, every act of faith nurtures the miracle hidden in God's plan for your life.

Your testimony has a conception, a beginning. Your breakthrough has a timeline. And your life, when aligned with God's Word, Spirit, and faith, will become undeniable evidence that God still works wonders.

Welcome to the birthplace of miracles. This is where the supernatural begins, where God speaks, the Spirit moves, and your faith positions you for what was once impossible to become your reality today.

THOUGHTS FOR REFLECTION

1. Which "seed" of God's Word are you holding onto right now?
2. How have you seen the Holy Spirit breathe life into a promise or situation in your past?
3. In what area of your life is God asking you to wait in faith, even when the outcome is not yet visible?
4. What step of obedience might God be prompting you to take that could move your miracle closer to manifestation?
5. How can you shift your perspective to see waiting not as wasted time, but as God's preparation?

PUT IT INTO PRACTICE

- *Plant the Seed:* Write down one promise from Scripture

that speaks to your situation. Let it take root in your heart this week.

- *Invite the Spirit*: Spend time in prayer asking the Holy Spirit to breathe fresh life into that promise. Be sensitive to His whispers and nudges.

- *Hold in Faith*: Each day, declare: "What God has spoken, He will perform." Remind yourself that unseen does not mean undone.

- *Act in Obedience*: Take one concrete step of obedience, however small, that aligns with God's Word over your life.

- *Persevere in Prayer*: Dedicate a set time this week to pray and "labor" for your promise until faith grows stronger than doubt.

Part Two
Purposes of the Miraculous

If we only see miracles as dramatic events, we miss their deeper meaning. Every miracle carries a message. They reveal who God is, confirm His Word, and align us with His greater plan. Miracles are not random interruptions in history but purposeful signs that declare God's love, glory, faithfulness, and calling.

In this section, we will uncover the divine purposes behind the miraculous. Each chapter will show that miracles are never ends in themselves. They are signposts pointing us back to God and forward to His promises. By understanding their purpose, we gain eyes to see that the miraculous is not about spectacle, but about revelation: revealing God's heart, His covenant, and His mission in the world.

4

Love, Power, and Glory in Miracles

"Biblical miracles have a clear objective: they are intended to bring the glory and love of God into bold relief. They are intended, among other things, to draw man's attention away from the mundane events of everyday life and direct it toward the mighty acts of God."

— Walter Elwell

Why does God work miracles? At the core, it is not simply to demonstrate His power but to reveal His heart. Every miracle is a window into His compassion, His faithfulness, and His desire to be close to His people. Miracles are not random acts; they are love in action, God reaching into human need with His care. From the pages of Scripture to the testimonies we hear today, miracles remind us that the God who created us has never abandoned us.

Miracles Prove God's Love

God performs miracles to show us His unchanging love. Some argue that miracles were limited to biblical times. But ask yourself: Does God still love and care for us? The answer is *absolutely.* The Bible tells us: *"Jesus Christ is the same yesterday, today, and forever."* (Hebrews 13:8) If His love has not changed, then neither has His willingness to work miracles.

Miracles are a tangible expression of God's ongoing involvement in His creation, His Church, and the lives of His people. While some claim God is distant or disconnected, miracles prove otherwise. Every miracle testifies that He is present and active. They show that He protects, delivers, defends, and blesses His people.

Miracles Reveal God's Glory and Nature

> *"And now, Father, glorify me in your presence with the glory I had with you before the world began."* (John 17:5)

Miracles are windows into God's heart and nature. They remind us that He is the Living God, our Provider, Healer, Protector, Deliverer, and Redeemer. In John 17:5, Jesus speaks of the eternal glory He shared with the Father, a glory that was manifested during His earthly ministry through miraculous works. Every healing, every deliverance, and every act of provision was more than compassion or power; it was a manifestation of divine glory, showing people who God is.

The psalmist declared: *"Our children will also serve him. Future*

50

generations will hear about the wonders of the Lord. His righteous acts will be told to those not yet born. They will hear about everything he has done" (Psalm 22:30–31, NLT). Miracles are not only for those who witness them; they are testimonies meant to be remembered, retold, and passed on.

Miracles Settle Controversies

Miracles have a way of silencing doubt. In the story of the ten plagues in Exodus 7:11-12:30, we see how God's supernatural power was demonstrated through Moses. His ministry in Egypt wasn't just about persuasive words. It was marked by supernatural signs that settled once and for all whether God had truly sent him.

When Pharaoh, in pride, dismissed God and refused to let His people go, God did not answer with debate but with undeniable miracles. In a culture where Pharaoh was worshiped as a god, the plagues demonstrated that Yahweh alone was supreme.

But it's also important to understand that not all that appears miraculous comes from God. Throughout history, people have encountered spiritual forces that can perform signs and wonders but are not from the Spirit of God. When Moses confronted Pharaoh, the Egyptian magicians were able to mimic some of the early miracles. They turned staffs into serpents and turned water to blood. But their power was limited. As the plagues grew more severe, they could not match them and were forced to admit defeat: *"This is the finger of God"* (Exodus 8:19).

These miracles were not only a sign of God's supremacy over Pharaoh but also a reassurance to His people. Each act of deliverance reminded Israel that their covenant-keeping God was present and active on their behalf. Miracles did more than defeat Egypt's false powers; they gave the Israelites courage to trust God in the face of fear and uncertainty. In the same way today, God still uses miracles to silence confusion, strengthen faith, and declare that His authority cannot be challenged.

Miracles are Christ-centered

Every miracle finds its true meaning in Jesus. He is the Bread of Life, the One who nourishes and sustains us (*John 6:35*). He is the Light of the world, the One who guides us out of darkness (*John 8:12*). He is the Resurrection and the Life, the One who conquers death and gives eternal life (*John 11:25*). If a miracle does not lead us back to Christ, it has failed in its purpose.

All signs converge at the cross and the empty tomb—the greatest wonders of history. From that empty tomb, the Kingdom broke into the world with power.

But not every supernatural sign is from God. Power alone is not enough to confirm something as divine. Even in the New Testament, Jesus warned: *"For false messiahs and false prophets will rise up and perform great signs and wonders so as to deceive, if possible, even God's chosen ones"* (*Matthew 24:24, NLT*). Paul also reminds us that Satan can masquerade as an angel of light (*2 Corinthians 11:14*).

That's why every miracle must be tested against the standard of Christ. Does it glorify Jesus? Does it affirm the truth of the gospel? Does it lead people closer to Him, or away from Him? True miracles have a Christ-centered nature. They demonstrate His authority and divine nature. They point people back to Him, not to human ego, superstition, or fear.

A miracle from God is not just an act of power for its own sake; it is a signpost to the Father's loving heart. To cultivate biblical faith for miracles, we must keep Jesus at the center. He is our foundation, our example, and our focus. Miracles aren't meant to make us famous, feed our pride, or entertain an audience. They are meant to reveal Christ and the Father's love to a broken world. When Jesus is lifted up, He draws all people to Himself (*John 12:32*). That is the true purpose of every genuine miracle.

Miracles as Faith Strengtheners

Miracles not only reveal God's love and glory, they also strengthen faith. When Lazarus stepped out of the tomb, *"many of the Jews who had come to visit Mary, and had seen what Jesus did, believed in Him"* (John 11:45). Miracles are hard to deny. They're tangible: you can see them, experience them, and feel their impact. They take faith from theory to testimony. It makes God real and personal. Each time God answers prayer in ways you know you could not arrange yourself, He invites you to trust Him more deeply.

Every true miracle, whether big or small, carries the unmistakable imprint of God's love and glory. They reveal His heart, affirm His supremacy, and call us to deeper faith. Yet miracles also do more than comfort us in our need. They point us toward something greater: the faithfulness of God's promises and the unfolding of His eternal plan.

To see this more clearly, we turn next to the prophetic nature of miracles, where signs and wonders serve not only as acts of love but also as declarations that God's Word and purposes will always come to pass.

THOUGHTS FOR REFLECTION

1. How have you personally experienced God's love and care in ways that felt miraculous, whether big or small?

2. When you think about the miracles in Scripture, which story most helps you see God's glory and nature revealed?

3. Do you sometimes find yourself believing in God's power but doubting His love or closeness to you personally? Why?

4. How can you test the miracles or answers to prayer you've witnessed against the standard of Christ? Do they glorify Him and draw you nearer to Him?

5. In what areas of your life do you need to be reminded that God is not distant but actively involved?

PUT IT INTO PRACTICE

Take time this week to notice the miracles, big and small, that show God's love and glory: your breath, your provision, your protection, or even an answered prayer.

Write down three specific ways you see His hand at work in your daily life. Then, choose one of them to share as a testimony with someone else.

As you testify of God's goodness, you not only encourage their faith but also anchor your own in the truth that every miracle finds its meaning in Christ, who is still at work in you today.

5

Miracles as Prophetic Signs

Miracles carry meaning beyond the moment. They point us back to God's promises and forward to His eternal plan. In Scripture, signs and wonders were not given merely to inspire awe. They were prophetic markers to confirm God's faithfulness and mark the unfolding of His purposes.

The same is true today. When God heals, restores, or provides in ways that defy human explanation, He is declaring the same message: *My Word stands. My covenant endures. My plan will not fail.* Miracles are both signs of what He has done and previews of what He is still bringing to pass.

Miracles Align Us with God's Purposes and Timing

God's miracles happen according to His perfect plan and timing. The Bible talks about *kairos* moments, which are specific, appointed times when God chooses to act to fulfill His divine plan and bring glory to His name.

When God promised to deliver Israel from Egypt (Exodus 3:9), He didn't do it randomly or on human terms. He performed signs and wonders exactly when they were needed: the plagues in Egypt, the parting of the Red Sea, the crossing of the Jordan, and the fall of Jericho. Each miracle moved His people forward at the right time, ensuring His promises came to pass.

The same is true of Jesus' birth. Long before it happened, Isaiah declared:

> *"Therefore the Lord himself will give you a sign: the virgin will conceive and give birth to a son, and will call him Immanuel."* (Isaiah 7:14, NKJV)

At the appointed moment, that prophecy was fulfilled in Mary, revealing that miracles do not happen randomly. They are precisely prepared to unfold in God's timing and to align us with His purposes.

Miracles as Prophetic Fulfillment

Miracles also serve as prophetic confirmations. They are signposts that God's Word is true and His promises will come to pass.

Throughout Scripture, miracles confirmed God's Word and His messengers. The miraculous birth of Isaac confirmed God's covenant promise to Abraham (Genesis 21:1–3). The plagues in Egypt and the parting of the Red Sea validated Moses' call and God's deliverance of His people (Exodus 14–16). In the New Testament, Jesus' healings and deliverances confirmed His identity as the promised Messiah (Luke 7:22; John 5:36).

Each miracle carried the same prophetic message: *"God's Word is true, and His promises will come to pass."* As Isaiah declared, *"My Word will not return to Me void, but it will accomplish what I please"*

(Isaiah 55:11).

Miracles also carry meaning beyond their immediate effect. They are a window into God's larger plan and reveal His eternal purposes of redemption, justice, and His glory among the nations. Elijah's fire on Mount Carmel was more than a dramatic display; it declared God's supremacy over false gods (1 Kings 18:36–39). And the resurrection of Jesus was the ultimate prophetic miracle, confirming God's plan of salvation and eternal life (1 Corinthians 15:20–22).

Even today, miracles continue this prophetic pattern. Every divine breakthrough, every answered prayer that defies human logic, is a continuation of God's prophetic narrative. Each miracle is not only a demonstration of power but a message from Heaven. It is a prophecy unfolding in real time.

Miracles Are Signs of God's Faithfulness

God is a faithful, promise-keeping God. He doesn't just think about us individually; He cares about generations too. The Bible assures us, *"He keeps His covenant of love for a thousand generations of those who love Him and keep His commandments"* (Deuteronomy 7:9).

In Scripture, a covenant is a binding promise or agreement between God and His people. It is more than a contract. It is a sacred relationship where God pledges His faithfulness, protection, and blessings to those who trust and obey Him. In return, His people commit to love, worship, and follow Him. Miracles often serve as visible reminders of these promises.

For example, when Hagar and her son Ishmael were lost in the desert, God heard Ishmael's cries and miraculously provided water (Genesis 21:14–19). Why? Because God had made a covenant with Ishmael's father, Abraham. God's faithfulness to

Abraham extended to his son, showing that He remembers His promises across generations.

Today, this truth remains the same. Every miracle is more than an act of power; it is a signpost of God's unshakable Word and His covenant faithfulness. From Abraham to Jesus, from the prophets to the apostles, God has always used miracles to confirm His promises and to point His people toward His greater plan of redemption. And He continues to do the same now. Each breakthrough, each answered prayer, is God reminding you: *My covenant is alive, My Word will not fail, My plan is unfolding.*

But miracles are not only about what God has done in the past. They are also invitations to position yourself for what He desires to do now. As you trust Him, you can be confident that every miracle, great or small, is part of His story being written in your life. When you align with the prophetic, you align with Heaven's timing, and miracles follow. The question is: Will you align your heart, your faith, and your obedience to receive it?

THOUGHTS FOR REFLECTION

1. How does seeing miracles as prophetic fulfillment change the way you understand them?
2. Which biblical miracle most strengthens your trust that God always keeps His Word?
3. Are there promises in Scripture you are still waiting to see fulfilled in your own life? How can remembering past miracles give you hope in the waiting?
4. Do you sometimes focus more on the miracle itself than on the God it points to?
5. How does knowing that miracles confirm God's covenant and mission inspire you to live with greater

expectancy?

PUT IT INTO PRACTICE

Choose one promise from Scripture that you believe God has spoken over your life. Write it down, and pray over it, asking the Holy Spirit to strengthen your faith and align your heart with God's timing. Each day, declare aloud: *"Your Word is true, and I believe You will bring it to pass."* Let this practice shift your focus from simply waiting for results to trusting the God who fulfills His promises.

6

Miracles and Divine Purpose

Miracles are never detached from purpose. They are not random displays of power, but intentional acts of God that reveal, confirm, and advance His assignments on earth. Every time God performs a miracle, it is connected to His greater plan, whether it is revealing who He is, equipping His servants, or validating the mission He has entrusted to them.

To understand miracles rightly, we must see them not only as blessings for personal benefit, but as signposts pointing to divine calling and responsibility.

Every Miracle Has an Assignment

Miracles are never casual or meaningless. Each one carries significance beyond the moment, tied to God's greater plan and assignment.

When Jesus healed the man born blind, He was not only restoring eyesight. He was declaring, *"I am the Light of the world"*

(John 9:5). When He fed the five thousand, He was pointing to Himself as the Bread of Life (John 6:35). In John's Gospel, every "I Am" statement is confirmed with a miracle that demonstrates it. None of these signs were incidental. Each one revealed His identity and validated His mission.

The same is true in the lives of ordinary people. Hannah prayed for years for a child and her request went unanswered, until she aligned her desire with God's purpose. When she vowed to dedicate her son to the Lord's service (1 Samuel 1:11), God opened her womb. Samuel was not just her child; he was God's chosen prophet to guide Israel (1 Samuel 3:20). Her miracle was granted when her prayer connected to God's assignment.

This reveals a principle many overlook: sometimes miracles remain delayed because we seek them only for personal fulfillment, without recognizing their connection to God's plan. It is like asking for a phone simply because we want one. But when God gives you that phone, He has a reason. It may be to empower you to fulfill your calling, extend your influence, or strengthen your ministry. Miracles are provisions for purpose.

Abraham and Sarah's story teaches the same truth. Isaac was not just the long-awaited child they desired, but the heir of God's covenant (Genesis 17:19; 21:1–3). Isaac represented what was born of the Spirit, not of human striving. Isaac was a promise fulfilled by God's power, unlike Ishmael, who was conceived through their attempt to "help" God's plan (Genesis 16:1–4). Paul explains this contrast: Ishmael was "born according to the flesh," while Isaac was "born through promise," a work of the Spirit (Galatians 4:22–23, 28–29; Romans 9:8). When we align our desires with God's assignment, we move from striving in the flesh to receiving by the Spirit.

Miracles are never ends in themselves. They are

confirmations of a call, alignments with divine timing, or empowerment for an assignment. When we pray for miracles without connecting them to God's purpose, we may miss their true significance.

Think of it like being given a company car. The car isn't provided for personal amusement but for the work you've been assigned to do. If it's misused, the privilege may be withdrawn. In the same way, when God releases miracles, He expects them to lead to greater obedience, service, and alignment with His purposes.

This understanding is critical. When the Israelites were delivered from Egypt, the purpose of the miracles was that they would have faith in God and that they would be spectacular display of power that would allow Pharaoh to release them into covenant service to God. When they later refused to honor that purpose, they forfeited blessings and faced judgment.

Every miracle, then, is an invitation into God's plan. To experience it fully, we must align our hearts with His purposes and assignments.

Miracles Validate God's Calling

Miracles are never detached from faith or mission; they are meant to follow those who truly belong to Christ. This is why Jesus declared, *"And these signs will follow those who believe…"* (Mark 16:17). God uses miracles to confirm His calling on a person's life. When He sends someone, He often backs their assignment with miraculous signs that demonstrate His authority and power.

Throughout Scripture, God used miracles to confirm His calling on those He chose and to demonstrate His power working through them. For example, He parted the Red Sea through Moses (Exodus 14:21–22), commanded the sun to stand still at Joshua's word (Joshua 10:12–14), and sent fire from heaven at Elijah's prayer on Mount Carmel (1 Kings 18:36–38).

Before the Israelites crossed the Jordan, God told Joshua, *"This day I will begin to exalt you in the eyes of all Israel so they may know that I am with you as I was with Moses"* (Joshua 3:7). He was making it clear that His miraculous power would validate Joshua's leadership.

When Jesus walked the earth, the Father used miracles to prove He was the Messiah (Acts 2:22). And when Jesus sent out His disciples, He anointed them to perform miracles so the world would know they were truly sent by Him.

Miracles are like a divine seal, a confirmation that God's presence and power are upon a person, validating their mission with the full backing of heaven.

THOUGHTS FOR REFLECTION

1. Have you ever prayed for a miracle without considering how it might connect to God's greater purpose?

2. How does Hannah's story challenge the way you pray for your own desires?

3. In what areas of your life might you be "striving in the flesh" rather than waiting for God to fulfill His promise by the Spirit?

4. How do the examples of Moses, Joshua, Elijah, and the disciples encourage you about God confirming His call through signs?

5. What assignments or responsibilities in your life could God be waiting to empower through a miracle?

PUT IT INTO PRACTICE

Take one area of your life where you are believing for a miracle, whether provision, healing, breakthrough, or guidance. Instead of only asking for the outcome, ask God to reveal the purpose behind it. Pray: *"Lord, show me how this miracle connects to Your calling and plan for my life. Align my heart with Your assignment so I can steward it well."*

Write down any insight or conviction the Holy Spirit gives you, and commit to respond in obedience. As you align your request with God's purpose, you open the door for Him to confirm His call and empower you for greater service.

Part Three
Positioning for the Miraculous

Miracles are the overflow of divine alignment, where God's sovereign will, the empowerment of the Holy Spirit, and the believing response of man intersect. Understanding miracles is only the beginning; the next step is learning how to posture ourselves to experience them.

Positioning for the miraculous is not about striving or persuading God to act. It means preparing our hearts to receive, removing hindrances that block His flow, and cultivating expectancy for Him to move. To walk in the miraculous, a believer must learn how to position himself spiritually, emotionally, and relationally so that God's power can flow without hindrance.

This section unpacks how we partner with God, cultivate the right atmosphere, and prepare the soil of our lives for supernatural manifestation. As you engage with these truths, you will see that miracles are not reserved for a chosen few but are available to all who align themselves with God's purposes and position their lives as vessels for His power and glory.

7

Faith and Expectation for Miracles

Every miracle begins with a posture. Not of striving, but of alignment with God's Word and His promises. Faith and expectation are two essential foundations of that alignment. Faith believes what God has spoken, and expectation prepares for its fulfillment. Together they create the atmosphere where God's power can move freely.

Throughout Scripture, this pattern repeats again and again: God speaks, His people believe, and faith-filled action follows. Whether it was Moses lifting his rod at the Red Sea, the widow gathering jars for oil, or the blind man crying out to Jesus, miracles came where faith and expectation converged.

In this chapter, we will explore how to cultivate both faith and expectation, not as abstract ideas, but as living postures that shape our prayers, decisions, and readiness for God's intervention.

Faith: The Foundation of the Miraculous

Faith is the seedbed of every miracle. Without faith, the soil of our hearts is not ready to receive what God desires to do. Scripture says plainly: *"And He did not do many miracles there because of their lack of faith"* (Matthew 13:58). Unbelief does not cancel God's presence, but it limits the manifestation of His power in our lives.

Faith is not a vague hope but a confident trust that God will do what He has promised. Paul writes: *"Faith comes by hearing, and hearing by the Word of God"* (Romans 10:17). Faith grows through the Word of God. Immersing ourselves in the Bible and reflecting on the miracles it records strengthens our faith and prepares us to receive our own miracles. Each promise of God becomes an anchor, rooting us in His character and reminding us that His Word cannot fail.

Faith also requires persistence. The blind man in Jericho refused to be silenced until Jesus restored his sight (Mark 10:46–52). His persistence activated his miracle. In the same way, faith presses through obstacles, silences voices of doubt, and clings to God's promises until they manifest.

But faith is not just believing. It is also acting. Moses had to lift his rod before the Red Sea parted. The widow had to gather jars before the oil multiplied. Faith demonstrates itself in obedience to God's Word, even when logic resists or circumstances seem impossible.

Growing Faith in Daily Life

Faith is something we can strengthen and grow. Below are practical ways to build your faith in everyday life:

- *Immerse in Scripture:* Reflect on God's promises and the miracles recorded in His Word until they sink into your heart.

- *Pray honestly:* Tell God your fears, doubts, and hopes. Ask Him to strengthen your faith. Faith isn't pretending there's no fear; it's choosing to trust God in the middle of it.

- *Declare the Word:* Speaking God's Word out loud builds confidence. It reminds you (and any doubt trying to take hold) of God's unchanging truth.

- *Remember past victories:* Take time to write or talk about times God has come through for you. Testimonies aren't just for others; they strengthen *your* faith, too.

- *Surround yourself with believers:* Community matters. Being around those who believe encourages you when your faith feels weak.

- *Worship:* Even when it feels hard. Worship shifts your focus from the problem to the Problem-Solver. It reminds you who God is.

A Testimony of Faith

I know this from personal experience. My wife's pregnancy with Miracle was anything but easy. She faced complications from the start with an incompetent cervix diagnosis that threatened to end everything prematurely.

When doctors told us our unborn baby wouldn't survive and urged us to end the pregnancy, my wife and I chose to hold onto God's promise instead. The doctors did their best to prepare us for the worst. They said that if the baby was delivered at that time, it would be too early and survival would be impossible.

When God speaks, His word is the final authority. So we refused to accept a hopeless prognosis. We prayed fervently. We declared that Miracle would live and not die, that she would proclaim the works of the Lord.

That decision to stand firm in faith, even in the face of frightening medical reports, positioned us to see God do the impossible. It wasn't easy, but our faith created the foundation for God to work in ways the doctors never expected.

Expectation: Preparing for the Promise

Expectation creates an environment where extraordinary things can happen. Faith believes, but expectation prepares. Faith says, *"God can."* Expectation says, *"God will, and I am ready."* Together, they create the atmosphere for breakthrough.

Expectation is never passive. It positions us not only to believe but to *receive*. Think of a pregnant woman. From the moment she knows she is expecting, she begins to prepare her home, body, and habits for the arrival of her child. In the same way, spiritual expectation shapes our actions, decisions, and mindset in anticipation of what God will do. It keeps us focused and prepared to see God's promises fulfilled. The difference between hope and expectation is preparation. Hope longs for change; expectation rearranges life to welcome it.

Nurturing Expectation in Practice

Expectation is not abstract; it is something we can cultivate intentionally in daily life. Here are some practical ways to nurture a posture of expectation:

- *Pray specifically:* Don't just ask God vaguely; name what you're believing for and write it down as a prayer request or faith statement. Specific prayers help focus your faith and make it easier to recognize God's answer when it comes.

- *Remove obstacles to your readiness:* Examine your heart and environment for anything that could hinder you from receiving what you're asking for. Ask God to help you develop the mindset and character that will allow you to receive and steward the miracle well when it comes.

- *Visualize the outcome:* Imagine what answered prayer would look like in your life. Picture yourself holding that baby, starting that new job, or living free from illness. This is not wishful thinking but expectation. Visualization moves your focus from the obstacle to the promise.

- *Take practical steps:* Show your expectation through action: buy baby clothes, update your résumé, plan for life after healing, or budget for provision. Preparation declares, *"I expect God to move."*

- *Stay alert for opportunities:* Expect God to move in unexpected ways, so you don't miss it when the door opens.

- *Give thanks in advance:* Thank God as if it's already done. Gratitude shifts your perspective from waiting to receiving.

A Testimony of Expectation

Before Miracle was born, God gave me her name in a dream. In that dream, I saw a beautiful little girl outside our home, and heard myself call to her: "Miracle, come to your dad."

That dream was not only a revelation; it became an anchor of expectation. It shaped our conviction that we would have a daughter and that she would live. It was the promise we held onto even in the darkest moments of the pregnancy. When circumstances looked impossible, when medical reports urged us to give up, that dream reminded us of God's word. It gave direction to our prayers, shifted the way we spoke about the pregnancy, and gave us the confidence to believe, not just for survival, but for full healing and life.

That's the power of expectation. It moves us from hoping to preparing, from waiting to getting ready, and from believing to doing. Expectation sets the stage for God to do what only He can do. And when paired with faith, the two become unstoppable. Faith lays the foundation, and expectation prepares the way. One without the other is incomplete. Faith believes God can, but expectation acts like He will. When faith and expectation converge, the atmosphere of our lives shifts, and miracles find a place to land.

THOUGHTS FOR REFLECTION

1. In what areas of your life do you find it hardest to believe God's promises? What holds back your faith?

2. How has Scripture in the past helped you build faith when circumstances seemed impossible?

3. What does active expectation look like for you at the moment? Are your actions aligned with what you are praying for?

4. Think about Hannah, the blind man in Jericho, or your own experiences—what role did persistence play in receiving the miracle?

5. How can gratitude and preparation demonstrate that you are expecting God to move?

PUT IT INTO PRACTICE

Choose one promise from Scripture that speaks directly to your current need. Write it down somewhere visible, whether on your phone, a mirror, or a notebook. Regularly:

-   Read it aloud and thank God in advance for fulfilling it.
-   Take practical steps that show your expectation (update a résumé, set aside money, prepare a space, or take another faith-filled action).
-   Keep a list of encouragements, confirmations, or small breakthroughs you notice along the way. As you continue this practice, reflect often on how it shifts your faith and expectation.

8

Spiritual Postures that Unlock the Miraculous

Positioning for miracles is not only about faith and expectation. While they both lay the foundation, spiritual postures sustain it and create the atmosphere where God's power can be revealed. These postures are not formulas or rituals but ways of walking with God. They are attitudes and disciplines that invite His presence and demonstrate our dependence on Him.

In this chapter, we will explore these spiritual postures not as burdens, but as pathways of alignment. They do not manipulate God into performing miracles; they prepare us to receive and steward what He chooses to release. A surrendered, aligned life is a life positioned for the miraculous.

Prayer and Fasting

Prayer and fasting are among the most powerful spiritual

postures that prepare us for the miraculous. Prayer is our invitation for God to intervene. Fasting deepens that invitation and shows our willingness to face physical challenges in a spiritual way. It is a tangible expression of humility and dependence on God.

Wherever you see God moving powerfully in a church, a family, or an individual life, you will often find a culture of prayer and fasting at the foundation. These are not ways to earn miracles through effort but ways of creating space in our hearts to hear God clearly and invite His intervention. When daily concerns crowd out these practices, it becomes harder to experience God's miraculous power.

Throughout the Bible, men and women who walked in the miraculous lived lives marked by prayer and fasting. Moses prayed forty days on the mountain until the glory of God changed his countenance (Exodus 34:28–29). Daniel fasted for twenty-one days, and heaven broke through with angelic help (Daniel 10:2–12). Even Jesus, before launching into His public ministry, fasted in the wilderness and returned in the power of the Spirit (Luke 4:1–14). These examples remind us that prayer and fasting are not optional extras. They are the lifeblood of a miracle-ready life.

Fasting helped these men and women of God stay focused on God and rely on His strength instead of their own. Some fasted for 21 or even 40 days, but fasting does not have to be long or extreme to be meaningful. It is not about the number of days you can endure. It is about the posture of your heart and your willingness to set aside comfort to focus on God. Even short fasts—such as skipping a meal, abstaining from certain foods, or stepping away from distractions like social media—can be spiritually significant when done in faith.

If you're medically unable to fast from food, you can still

practice fasting by abstaining from something else that takes your time and attention, dedicating that space to prayer, worship, and listening to God.

The goal is always the same: to humble ourselves before God, seek Him with all our hearts, and invite His power into our circumstances. Fasting and prayer together say, "God, I need You more than anything else."

A Story of Bold Faith

It is easy to talk about miracles and long for them, but true spiritual hunger requires us to *act* on what we believe. That is why I love the example of Archbishop Benson Idahosa. Early in his walk with God, he had a burning curiosity about the supernatural. One day, he approached his pastor with a question:

"I read in the Bible that, 'In My name, you'll cast out devils, heal the sick, and raise the dead.' Who said that?"

His pastor replied, "Jesus did."

Idahosa, eager for understanding, pressed further, "Do you believe it?"

"Yes," the pastor answered.

"Have you done it?" Idahosa asked.

The pastor hesitated and finally admitted that he had not.

"Can I do it?" Idahosa asked after a thoughtful pause.

With a mixture of encouragement and curiosity, the pastor replied, "Yes, you can."

"If Jesus said it, and I can do it," Idahosa declared with conviction, "then I will try."

He went out boldly into his community, knocking on doors and asking if anyone had died. Eventually, he found a grieving family. When he asked if he could pray, they agreed. As he prayed, God raised the child. In time, throughout his ministry, Idahosa would go on to raise several others from the dead.

This story challenges us: Are we willing to go beyond talking about God's power and actually partner with Him to see it? Prayer and fasting are not magic formulas. They are ways to draw closer to God, hear His voice more clearly, and create room for His miraculous intervention.

A Personal Testimony

I remember when my wife's pregnancy with Miracle took a serious turn. The doctors discovered that her cervix had reopened after an initial procedure to sew it shut, and she would need another emergency cerclage to try to prevent preterm delivery. This second procedure was far more complex than the first. In fact, the doctors admitted there were three major complications they had never faced together in a single case.

They were willing to attempt the surgery, but made it clear they could not guarantee the outcome. We knew this was beyond human ability. In those critical days, my wife and I cried out to God in prayer. We poured out our hearts out to Him, asking not just for a successful procedure, but for a miracle.

When the day of the surgery finally came, we placed everything in God's hands. Afterward, the surgeon came back and told us it was the easiest and smoothest procedure she had ever performed, even though it had been one of the most complex. Prayer had created the space for God to do what we could not.

No matter who you are, you can seek God in this way. It is not about being a pastor or a spiritual "expert." It is about cultivating a heart that says, "God, use me." It is about having the courage to act on His promises and believe that He still works wonders today.

Worship and Gratitude

Worship is one of the most powerful postures for inviting the miraculous. At its core, worship is not about music or ritual but about honoring and reverencing God for who He is. It magnifies Him above every problem and reminds us that He is greater than any obstacle we face. Gratitude flows out of worship, creating an atmosphere of faith where impossibilities lose their power.

Scripture gives us vivid pictures of how worship shifts the atmosphere. When the Israelites faced battles they couldn't win on their own, they often sent worshipers ahead of the army. In 2 Chronicles 20, when Jehoshaphat faced a vast army, he sent singers to the front lines. As they praised the Lord, God set ambushes against their enemies and gave them the victory.

In Acts 16, Paul and Silas prayed and sang hymns while chained in prison. As they lifted their voices, a violent earthquake shook the foundations of the prison, doors flew open, and every chain came loose. In both cases, worship created space for heaven to intervene.

Why does worship carry such power in the miraculous? Worship magnifies God and lifts His name above every fear. Choosing to worship in bleak or hopeless moments silences fear and renews hope. When God becomes bigger in your eyes, your situation begins to shrink—not always immediately in the physical, but first in your heart. That shift in perspective is where victory begins, even before the battle is over.

You do not wait to worship until the problem is gone. You worship in spite of it. You speak what God has said, declare His promises, and thank Him for His faithfulness before the answer comes. Honoring God with sincere worship and a heart aligned to Him opens the door for His power to be revealed.

But worship is not limited to singing or praising with our lips. It is also expressed in the way we honor God with our resources. Sacrificial giving declares, "God, I trust You more than I trust what is in my hand."

Giving to God, and to the things He cares about—whether through offerings, supporting His work, or helping those in need—draws His attention and opens the door for miraculous provision. Proverbs 19:17 says, *"Whoever is kind to the poor lends to the Lord, and He will reward them for what they have done."* Acts of generosity are more than charity; they are invitations for God to move on our behalf.

In Scripture, sacrificial giving often came before divine intervention. For example, the widow of Zarephath gave her last bit of flour and oil to Elijah during a famine, and in return, her jar never emptied and her jug never ran dry (1 Kings 17:8–16).

Worship is not limited to a church service or a song; it is a lifestyle. Every time you exalt God in the face of fear, give thanks instead of complain, or give sacrificially when it costs you something, you are positioning yourself for a miracle. Worship shifts the atmosphere, gratitude prepares the heart, and together they invite God's power to be revealed.

Holiness and Consecration

Holiness is not about perfection but about separation. It is setting ourselves apart for God's purposes. To consecrate your life is to say, "Lord, I belong to You. My thoughts, words, and actions are Yours." When our lives are yielded to Him, we create an atmosphere where His power can move freely.

Throughout Scripture, holiness and miracles often go hand in hand. Before Israel could enter the Promised Land, Joshua told the people, *"Consecrate yourselves, for tomorrow the Lord will do amazing things among you"* (Joshua 3:5). The call to holiness came before the miracle of the Jordan River parting. Likewise, in the New Testament, the apostles walked in great power because they lived lives surrendered to the Holy Spirit, avoiding anything that would grieve Him (Acts 5:12–16).

Though miracles are gifts of grace, holiness creates consistency. Sin, compromise, and divided loyalty dull our sensitivity to God and can hinder His power from being revealed. Consecration, on the other hand, sharpens our focus, deepens intimacy with God, and keeps us aligned with His will. As Peter reminds us, *"But just as He who called you is holy, so be holy in all you do; for it is written: 'Be holy, because I am holy'"* (1 Peter 1:15–16).

Holiness is not legalism or rule-keeping but a posture of love: choosing to honor Him above all else. To walk in holiness is to live in continual surrender. It is allowing God to purify your motives, renew your mind, and align your actions with His Word. The more we yield to Him, the more His presence fills our lives. And where His presence is, miracles follow.

Forgiveness

Unforgiveness can block us from experiencing God's power, including miracles. The Bible teaches that forgiveness is not only a command but an essential posture for receiving His blessings and intervention. Jesus makes this clear in Matthew 6:14–15: *"For if you forgive other people when they sin against you, your heavenly Father will also forgive you. But if you do not forgive others their sins, your Father will not forgive your sins.*

This principle extends beyond salvation. When we refuse to forgive, we close ourselves off to God's grace and mercy, the very things we need for miracles to happen. Bitterness and resentment act like barriers that hinder the flow of His power.

Jesus also linked forgiveness directly to prayer and faith:

"Therefore I tell you, whatever you ask for in prayer, believe that you have received it, and it will be yours. And when you stand praying, if you hold anything against anyone, forgive them, so that your Father in heaven may forgive you your sins" (Mark 11:24–25).

Holding on to anger or grudges makes prayer less effective. It hardens our hearts and makes it difficult for God's love and power to work freely in us. Unforgiveness keeps us spiritually stuck, trapped in the past instead of moving forward into all God has prepared.

Forgiveness, on the other hand, lifts that weight and opens our hearts to God's miraculous power. Choosing to forgive shows faith in His justice and trust in His ability to deal with what was done to us. That trust creates space for His intervention and allows His power to flow unhindered in our lives. And if forgiveness feels impossible, ask God for help. He understands your pain and will give you the grace to release it.

Service and Testimony

Serving God is one of the most overlooked postures that prepares us for the miraculous. When we devote our time, energy, and resources to His Kingdom, we position ourselves under His favor.

Service is not a transaction to earn blessings. It is an expression of love and loyalty to the One who has already given us everything. Yet Scripture shows that God often honors faithful service with divine intervention.

When King Hezekiah was told through the prophet Isaiah that his illness would lead to death, he prayed and reminded God of his wholehearted service (Isaiah 38:3). He had served God faithfully by leading Judah back to true worship, removing idols, trusting God during crises like the Assyrian invasion, and refusing to rely on foreign alliances for rescue. His leadership was marked by sincere and consistent devotion to God. In response, the Lord heard his prayer, healed him, and added fifteen more years to his life.

In much the same way, your service in God's house creates a history of faithfulness with Him. Even when no one else notices, God does. And when you face impossible situations, that faithful history can become a platform for breakthrough.

This was true for me even during our most difficult season in the hospital with Miracle, when she was in the NICU. In those long, painful days, I made a choice to serve God by encouraging other parents who were walking through the same struggles, both in the NICU and those still believing God for children of their own. I would share what helped us: teaching them how to pray, trust God, and speak His Word.

Serving others in the middle of our crisis was one way of staying faithful to what God had called me to do. It became a source of strength and a foundation for asking Him to intervene powerfully on our behalf.

Just as service prepares the way, testimony multiplies the impact of God's miracles. In Acts 3, when the lame man at the gate Beautiful was healed, he leapt and praised God, and the whole city took notice. His testimony became a seed that ignited faith in others. Revelation 12:11 declares that believers *"overcame him by the blood of the Lamb and by the word of their testimony."*

Sharing what God has done not only strengthens your own faith but also creates expectation in the hearts of others.

Testimony is a form of service. It points people back to God, honors His work, and invites Him to do it again.

Every time you serve and every time you testify, you are positioning yourself and others to encounter the miraculous. Service roots you in God's purposes, and testimony spreads His power beyond you. Together, they make your life a vessel through which heaven touches earth.

Covenant Relationship with God

Our relationship with God is one of the most important conditions for experiencing miracles. While He may at times show grace and perform miracles for anyone, the clearest and most consistent flow of His power is found in covenant relationship with Him.

Israel experienced countless miracles, not because they were more deserving, but because God had made a covenant with Abraham. He promised to make his descendants a great nation, give them a land of their own, and be their God forever (Genesis 12:2–3; 15:18; 17:7). Because of that covenant, God delivered them from Egypt, parted the Red Sea, defeated their enemies, provided water from a rock, and sent manna from heaven. Each miracle flowed out of His faithfulness to His promise.

Through Christ, we too become partakers of this covenant. Paul writes, *"If you belong to Christ, then you are Abraham's seed, and heirs according to the promise"* (Galatians 3:29). By faith, we are adopted into God's family and share in His covenant blessings. The same God who delivered, provided, and fought for Israel is committed to us as well. His covenant faithfulness continues today in the lives of all who belong to Him.

Outside of a covenant relationship, other spiritual forces may demonstrate signs or wonders, but only God brings lasting healing, deliverance, and transformation. True miracles are rooted in His love and faithfulness. When we walk with Him, we create space for His power to move, not through formulas or superstition, but through intimacy with the One who performs true miracles.

Yet God's love is so great that even those outside covenant can still experience His miracles. The Canaanite woman who begged Jesus to heal her daughter received her miracle through persistent faith, even though she was outside Israel's covenant (Matthew 15:26–28). Her story shows that faith draws God's attention and opens the door to His intervention.

Covenant relationship with God is the ultimate posture for the miraculous. Prayer, fasting, worship, holiness, forgiveness, service, and testimony all flow from it. These practices are not ends in themselves but expressions of a life anchored in Him. When relationship is the foundation, miracles shift from rare interruptions to natural overflow.

THOUGHTS FOR REFLECTION

1. In what ways have you experienced your faith or expectation shaping the atmosphere for God to move?

2. How do prayer and fasting help you shift your focus from yourself to God?

3. When circumstances feel overwhelming, what would it look like for you to magnify God through worship and gratitude instead of magnifying the problem?

4. Are there areas of compromise where God is calling you to deeper holiness and consecration?

5. Is unforgiveness hindering your prayers or your ability to receive God's power?

6. How can your service in God's house or your personal testimony create space for others to experience the miraculous?

PUT IT INTO PRACTICE

- *Build Faith Daily:* Meditate on God's promises, confess His Word out loud, and remember past victories (Romans 10:17).
- *Pursue Prayer and Fasting:* Dedicate regular time to seek God's face, even in small ways, to realign your heart with Him (Daniel 10:2–12; Luke 4:1–14).
- *Worship and Give Thanks:* Choose praise over complaint. Thank God before you see the answer (2 Chronicles 20:21; Acts 16:25).
- *Walk in Holiness:* Guard your heart, repent quickly, and keep yourself sensitive to God's Spirit (Joshua 3:5; 1 Peter 1:15–16).
- *Forgive Freely:* Release offenses, trusting God with justice, so your prayers remain unhindered (Mark 11:25).
- *Serve and Testify:* Find one way this week to serve in God's Kingdom, and share a testimony of His goodness to encourage someone else (Acts 3:8–10; Revelation 12:11).

9

God's Timing for Miracles

From the very beginning, Scripture reveals a God who moves with precision. He performs His miracles at appointed times and specific seasons. These times are part of His larger plan.

Creation itself began with God speaking light into darkness at the exact moment He chose. The exodus of Israel unfolded when the years of captivity were complete. The coming of Christ was described as happening "in the fullness of time" (Galatians 4:4). From Genesis to Revelation, the message is consistent: God makes all things beautiful in His time (Ecclesiastes 3:11).

Miracles are part of God's timetable. They are specific moments when heaven intersects earth to reveal His glory, fulfill His promises, and advance His purposes. Sometimes these miracles arrive in their appointed season. At other times, faith and desperation draw them into the present. Either way, timing is central, and to understand the miraculous we must learn to recognize God's seasons and align ourselves with His timing.

Chronos vs. Kairos

The Bible uses two different words for time: *chronos* and *kairos*. Chronos is ordinary, measurable time. It represents the steady passing of hours, days, and years. It is the kind of time that keeps calendars and clocks, the time we count and manage in daily life.

Kairos, however, is different. It speaks of God's appointed, divinely chosen moments, specific seasons when heaven breaks into history to fulfill a purpose. Chronos counts the minutes, but kairos counts the miracles.

When God parted the Red Sea, it did not happen the instant Israel was trapped. It happened at the precise kairos moment, when His glory would be revealed, Pharaoh humbled, and His people delivered.

When Jesus came into the world, Paul described it as happening "in the fullness of time" (Galatians 4:4). Kairos moments are when eternity touches time, and God's purposes advance in ways no human effort could arrange.

This truth encourages us when miracles seem delayed. They are not forgotten. They are waiting for the moment God has set. Our responsibility is not to manipulate His timing but to stay sensitive, alert, and ready to step into the season when He moves.

In-Season and Out-of-Season Miracles

When we talk about the timing for miracles, it helps to understand the difference between *in-season* and *out-of-season* miracles. In-season miracles happen during times of God's special visitation. These are appointed moments He has set aside to accomplish specific purposes. They take place in alignment with His timing and will.

Zacharias and Elizabeth had prayed for years to have a child, but God had a specific plan that connected John's birth with the birth of Jesus. This fulfilled the prophecy that John would prepare the way for the Messiah (Luke 1:13-17). The timing of John's birth was intentional and part of God's greater purpose.

In the same way, Lazarus was raised only after four days in the tomb, even though Jesus loved Lazarus and His disciples wanted Him to act immediately. This delay was not because Jesus did not care, but because the timing was important for revealing God's glory and fulfilling His purpose. Sometimes God allows time to pass so that the circumstances are ready for the miracle and so His perfect will can be accomplished.

Another picture of in-season miracles is found at the Pool of Bethesda, where healing came only at the specific time when the angel stirred the water (John 5:3–4). The miracle was tied to a specific moment chosen by God.

Each of these miracles was tied to a season on God's calendar. They did not arrive early or late, but at the precise moment His purposes required. As the psalmist declares, *"You will arise and have mercy on Zion; for the time to favor her, yes, the set time, has come"* (Psalm 102:13).

Out-of-season miracles, on the other hand, are interventions God grants outside the expected or appointed season for a matter. They do not overturn His sovereignty; rather, they are responses to persistent faith, urgent need, and humble petition.

At the wedding in Cana, Jesus turned water into wine even though He said His time had not yet come. A need was presented, faith was expressed, and He responded (John 2:1–11). Likewise, the Syrophoenician woman, though outside the covenant, persisted in asking for her daughter's healing. Her determined faith drew a miracle into the present (Matthew 15:21–28).

These examples reveal a God who is sovereign yet

responsive. He has appointed seasons for His power to be displayed, but He is also moved by genuine faith and urgent need. When God's timing meets our trust in Him, the result is a divine moment where heaven touches earth.

Divine Appointments

Miracles also occur through divine appointments, which are moments when God aligns people, places, and circumstances in ways that no human planning could achieve. These are not coincidences but heaven's setups, orchestrated to reveal His glory at just the right time.

The woman with the issue of blood had carried her condition for twelve years, but her healing came in a single encounter when she pressed through the crowd to touch the hem of Jesus' garment (Mark 5:25–34). The lame man who sat daily at the Beautiful Gate of the temple met Peter and John on the very day God had ordained his healing, and his restored strength became a testimony to all who knew him (Acts 3:1–10).

Divine appointments remind us that timing is not only about seasons but also about readiness. God arranges intersections where faith meets opportunity, and lives are transformed. Our part is to stay spiritually alert, sensitive to His leading, and willing to respond when He opens the door. What may look like an ordinary moment can become the stage for the extraordinary when it has been prepared by God.

Lessons from History

God's timing for miracles is not only seen in Scripture but also echoed throughout recent history. Take Oral Roberts. As a young man, he battled severe tuberculosis, an illness that threatened his life and future. In that place of weakness, God met him and called him into ministry. Despite his health challenges, he trusted God's call. And he experienced healing that changed the course of his life. That miracle became the foundation of a ministry that touched millions, helped ignite a global awareness of God's healing power, and founded a university dedicated to raising up new leaders for Christ.

Another example is David Yonggi Cho. He was born into a Buddhist family in Korea and battled sickness that left him without hope. After encountering Christ and receiving healing, he dedicated his life to God, eventually planting and leading one of the largest churches in the world. His life is a testimony of how God can transform someone with no Christian background into a mighty vessel for His purposes.

Kenneth Hagin's story is similar. He was born with a deformed heart and an incurable blood disease, and doctors told him he would not live past his teenage years. Yet as he read and believed the promises of Scripture, he was completely healed, and his testimony sparked decades of teaching on faith and healing that influenced believers worldwide.

These stories remind us that God's timing is not confined to the past. He still moves in both appointed seasons and unexpected moments, raising up ordinary men and women whose lives testify to His faithfulness. What unites these examples is not human strength or qualification but simple availability. God looks for hearts willing to trust Him, to say yes, and to step forward when His timing opens the door.

Aligning with God's Timing

If miracles are tied to God's timing, how do we align ourselves with those moments? Alignment begins in the posture of the heart. It means living with readiness to hear His voice, willingness to act when He speaks, and surrender to move when He calls. Miracles are not forced by human striving, but they are often released when faith meets the season God has prepared.

Sometimes the breakthrough comes not in dramatic displays of power but in the quiet strength of obedience. A single yielded *yes* can become the meeting place of eternity and time, the moment where heaven touches earth. The key is trust and believing that God's timing is never too early or too late, but always perfect.

When the heart is surrendered, the moment is aligned, and the miracle manifests. Not late, not early, but perfectly within God's appointed season.

THOUGHTS FOR REFLECTION

1. How does understanding the difference between *chronos* and *kairos* reshape the way you view God's timing?
2. Which biblical example of an in-season miracle most strengthens your trust that God's plans always unfold at the right time?
3. Have you ever experienced what felt like an out-of-season miracle—an unexpected breakthrough that came through persistent faith?
4. What "ordinary" moments in your life might actually be divine appointments waiting for you to recognize them?
5. How can remembering testimonies from history (both biblical and modern) stir your faith to trust God's timing in your own journey?

PUT IT INTO PRACTICE

Write down one area where you sense God may be preparing an appointed time for breakthrough. Then pray, *"Lord, align my heart with Your timing. Help me to be ready, watchful, and willing to respond when You move."*

10

In His Time: Delay, Timing, and God's Greater Plan

Few seasons test our faith more than waiting. We pray, we believe, and we hold on to God's promises, yet time passes and the answer does not appear. In those moments, it can feel as if heaven is silent or as if God has forgotten. Yet Scripture assures us that this is never the case. Delay is not denial. What may feel like a pause is often God's way of aligning His purposes, shaping our character, and preparing us to carry the miracle when it comes.

This chapter explores the mystery of waiting. We will look at seasons of preparation, the difference between delay and denial, and how to align ourselves with God's appointed timing. Through it all, one assurance remains—your miracle will not come late. It will come in God's perfect time.

And finally, we will face a difficult but liberating truth:

sometimes God says no, not to punish us, but to redirect us into a purpose greater than we imagined.

Seasons of Preparation

Waiting is never wasted. In God's economy, it is God's workshop of preparation. Delay is often the classroom where He shapes character, deepens faith, and equips us for the promise ahead. What feels like silence is often the unseen work of God preparing us to carry the very miracle we're longing for.

Joseph's story shows this clearly. He received dreams of leadership as a teenager, yet spent years in slavery and prison before Pharaoh's summons lifted him into destiny (Genesis 37–41). Those years of obscurity were not punishment but preparation, teaching him humility, resilience, and wisdom that would sustain him once the miracle of promotion came.

Moses likewise spent forty years in the desert before leading Israel out of Egypt (Exodus 2:15; Acts 7:30). The wilderness stripped away self-reliance and gave him an encounter with God at the burning bush. That shaped him into a deliverer who leaned on divine strength instead of human ability.

David was anointed king as a young shepherd boy but he still had to spend years fleeing Saul before ascending the throne (1 Samuel 16 – 2 Samuel 5). The waiting seasons refined his character, birthed psalms of worship, and taught him to depend on God as his refuge and fortress.

These delays were not wasted time but divine shaping. They reveal that God is less interested in rushing us into a miracle than in readying us to sustain it. Without preparation, a blessing can quickly become a burden. But when we allow waiting to do its work, the miracle arrives into hands that are steady, hearts that are humble, and lives that are aligned with God's purposes.

Waiting, then, is not passivity but active alignment. It is a season where faith is tested, endurance is formed, and vision is sharpened. Every delay becomes an investment into the strength and maturity required for the miracle to last.

Delay vs. Denial

One of the greatest challenges in the life of faith is learning to distinguish between God's *delay* and His *denial*. When prayers go unanswered, it is easy to assume God has said no. Yet very often, the silence we experience is not refusal but timing. Delay tests our faith, but it does not mean God has abandoned His promise.

Abraham and Sarah knew this tension well. God promised them a child, but decades passed before Isaac was born (Genesis 21:1–3). Their waiting was not a sign of God's neglect; it was a stage set for His power to be displayed. Isaac's birth in their old age showed beyond doubt that the child was not the result of human effort but the fulfillment of God's word.

Joseph also endured delay. God gave him dreams of greatness, but instead of immediate fulfillment, he was sold into slavery, falsely accused, and imprisoned (Genesis 37–41). The delay was not denial; it was God's preparation. When the appointed moment came, Joseph stepped into leadership with the maturity forged in adversity.

David's anointing as king did not lead straight to the throne. Years of waiting, hiding, and hardship refined him into the man who would shepherd Israel with integrity and dependence on God (2 Samuel 5:3–4).

Even in the New Testament, we see this principle in action. When Jesus heard that Lazarus was sick, He delayed His visit deliberately. The waiting ended not in death's triumph but in resurrection glory (John 11:4–6, 43–44).

These stories remind us that God's delays are never wasted. They are purposeful pauses that align circumstances, refine character, and display His glory in ways immediate answers never could.

When you face waiting, don't assume God has rejected your prayer. Instead, trust that He is working behind the scenes, weaving together His timing, your growth, and the circumstances that will allow the miracle to come forth in fullness.

God's Perfect Timing

If there is one truth Scripture affirms again and again, it is that God's timing is flawless. He is never late, though His ways may test our patience and stretch our faith. What feels like delay to us is often divine orchestration, where God carefully arranges moments so that His glory is revealed at the right place, the right time, and through the right vessel.

The story of Samson's mother highlights this truth with striking clarity. For years she lived with the ache of barrenness, carrying unfulfilled longing in her heart. But at the very time when Israel was crying out under the heavy oppression of the Philistines, God moved. The angel of the Lord appeared to her with a message that was not only personal but national in scope: she would conceive a son who would begin to deliver Israel (Judges 13:1–5).

Samson's birth was divinely timed to answer the prayers of a nation and to fulfill God's covenant purposes. So intentional was this miracle that God sent His angel not once, but twice, to give specific instructions on how the child was to be raised. Samson was to be set apart as a Nazirite from birth, dedicated wholly to God's service. Even before he was conceived, his life had a calling, and his parents were entrusted with the sacred responsibility of preparing him for it.

This reminds us that waiting is often purposeful. Samson's mother may have longed for a child years earlier, but God's plan required that her son be born at the exact moment Israel needed a deliverer. What felt like delay was, in reality, perfect orchestration. The miracle was not late. It came precisely when it was meant to, fulfilling both a personal longing and a national purpose.

God's timing is rarely our timing, but it is always intentional. We may not always understand the pauses, but when the miracle manifests, it becomes clear that the waiting was not wasted. In His appointed season, God fulfills His word with precision, power, and perfect faithfulness.

When God Says No

Not every prayer ends with the answer we hoped for. Sometimes, despite our faith and persistence, God says no. This can be one of the hardest realities to accept, especially when the request feels pure and deeply personal. Yet even in the no, God's love and wisdom remain. His denial is not rejection. It is sometimes redirection toward a higher purpose we may not yet see.

As we just saw in the story of Samson's mother, she waited years for her prayer to be answered, and God fulfilled it when the time was right. But not every woman in Israel had the same story. Some remained barren. Some longed for children of their own but never carried them. Yet many of these women were entrusted with another kind of legacy: to become spiritual mothers and nurturers to many. Their barrenness was not the end of their fruitfulness; it was the soil where God planted a different kind of purpose.

Anna the prophetess is a powerful example. She was a widow, and Scripture gives no record of children. Yet she devoted herself to worship, prayer, and fasting in the temple (Luke 2:36–38). It was Anna who recognized the infant Jesus as the promised Messiah and proclaimed His arrival to all who were waiting for redemption. Though she may never have experienced the family life she once desired, her faithfulness positioned her to play a key role in the story of salvation.

My own family carries such a story. My great-grandmother's sister, who could not have children of her own, chose to raise her sister's child as her own. She poured faith, love, and godly instruction into that life, creating a foundation that would impact generations. I am a beneficiary of the godly heritage she passed down, and today I am able to impact lives for Christ because of it. Her inability to bear children did not diminish her influence; it multiplied it, leaving a legacy that continues to touch countless lives for God's glory.

Pharaoh's daughter provides another example. She did not give birth to Moses, yet she raised him as her son. Because of her decision, Israel's deliverer was preserved and prepared for his calling (Exodus 2:5–10). In the same way, God sometimes entrusts us with purposes and people we did not expect, calling us to mother, father, or shepherd beyond the boundaries of our own plans.

It is tempting to believe that God's no means He has forgotten us. But in reality, His no often hides a greater yes. Sometimes the miracle we long for does not come because God is positioning us for a different assignment, one that will bear fruit in ways we could not have imagined.

Paul reminds us, *"We know in part and we prophesy in part"* (1 Corinthians 13:9). On this side of eternity, some questions will remain unanswered. Many of us know someone who believed for healing and still passed away, or someone who prayed earnestly for provision, reconciliation, or breakthrough that never seemed to come. These moments can shake our faith and leave us wondering why God did not intervene. But Scripture assures us that unanswered prayers are not evidence of God's absence or indifference. They are mysteries wrapped in His sovereignty and reminders that His perspective reaches beyond what we can see in this life.

One day, in eternity, we will understand fully what now we only glimpse in part (1 Corinthians 13:12). Until then, we cling to the truth that His character is good, His wisdom is perfect, and His love never fails.

When God says no, it is not the end of the story. It is an invitation to trust Him more deeply, to look beyond our own desires, and to embrace the higher purpose He is writing through our lives.

THOUGHTS FOR REFLECTION

1. How do you usually respond when what you're praying for seems delayed? What emotions or thoughts rise up in you?

2. Looking at Samson's story, how does it encourage you to believe that God's timing is both personal and purposeful?

3. Have you ever experienced a situation where God's "no" later made sense in light of a greater plan? How did that shape your faith?

4. Which of the stories in this chapter (Samson's mother, Anna the prophetess, Pharaoh's daughter, or the family

testimony) most speaks to your own struggles with waiting or unanswered prayer? Why?

5. What does it mean for you personally to live in the tension of *"we know in part"* (1 Corinthians 13:9) while still trusting that God is good and faithful?

PUT IT INTO PRACTICE

- *Surrender the timing:* Write down one prayer or desire that feels delayed. Instead of asking God *"when,"* ask Him to help you trust His timing. Declare Ecclesiastes 3:11 over it: *"He has made everything beautiful in its time."*

- *Reframe a "no":* Think of one area in your life where God has not answered the way you hoped. Ask Him to show you the bigger purpose He may be writing through it. Pray for grace to accept and walk in that purpose.

- *Step into legacy:* Consider one way you can impact others even if your own desires are not yet fulfilled—whether mentoring, serving, or caring for someone God brings across your path. Sometimes your influence in another person's life is the very miracle God wants to release through you.

11

Keeping Your Miracle Alive

Can miracles be lost? How do you keep a miracle alive after you've received it? It's one thing to receive a miracle, but it's another to keep it. A person can receive a miraculous breakthrough only to see it "die" over time. Learning how to protect and sustain what God has given you is just as important as receiving it in the first place.

In many ways, this is like the world of sports. Winning a title is an incredible achievement, but defending it is an entirely different challenge. A heavyweight boxing champion or an Olympic gold medalist may hold the title for a time, but sooner or later, they must defend it against challengers.

It's the same with miracles. They are not just one-time events. They are gifts, blessings, and divine interventions that require faith not just to receive but also to sustain. Just as athletes train, prepare, and fight to retain their status, we must be intentional about protecting and preserving the miracles God has entrusted to us.

The story of the Shunammite woman in 2 Kings 4:8–37 is a powerful example of this principle, showing us that even a miracle can be lost, and how God, through faith, can restore it.

Lessons from the Shunammite Woman

The Shunammite woman had no children, and her husband was old, but God performed a miracle through the prophet Elisha. He prophesied that she would have a son, and the following year, she did.

Years later, tragedy struck when the boy suddenly fell ill and died. Yet even in her grief, the woman did not give up. She went straight back to Elisha, convinced that the same God who gave her the miracle could also preserve it. She shows us that keeping a miracle alive requires the same faith, trust, and determination it took to receive it in the first place.

Sadly, many people will press in with everything they have to obtain a miracle, only to neglect the vigilance required to keep it. If we want God's blessings to endure, we must be just as intentional in protecting them as we were in receiving them. The faith and prayer that brought the miracle must continue after it arrives.

We must also remember that miracles don't remove us from spiritual warfare. Jesus warned that the enemy comes *"to steal, kill, and destroy"* (John 10:10), and Peter reminds us that he prowls around like a roaring lion, seeking someone to devour (1 Peter 5:8). Receiving your miracle is a victory, but it doesn't mean the battle is over. That is the moment to guard your heart, stay close to God, and remain steadfast in faith. When we do, we are equipped to resist the enemy's schemes and hold fast to the victory Christ has already won.

Sustaining Your Miracle Through Divine Relationships

One of the most critical ways to preserve a miracle is by valuing the relationships God used to release it. We live in a generation where people often take relationships for granted, receiving what they want and then quickly moving on. Offense, neglect, or spiritual attack can easily break these ties. But divine connections are not disposable. They are often the very channels through which God's blessing continues to flow.

We see in the story of the Shunammite woman that when her promised son died, she did not turn away in bitterness or despair. Instead, she went back to Elisha, the prophet who had first spoken God's promise. Because she honored and maintained that relationship, she was able to seek restoration, and God brought her miracle back to life. Her faith and loyalty to the connection God had placed in her life preserved what the enemy tried to steal.

Many lose their miracles by cutting themselves off from the very people God used to bless them. The Shunammite woman shows another way. By honoring Elisha, she positioned herself for restoration, and even beyond her lifetime her family continued to reap the favor of that relationship (2 Kings 8:1–6).

If we want miracles to last, we must steward God-given relationships with wisdom and humility. These connections often carry ongoing favor, provision, and restoration far beyond a single breakthrough. To protect your miracle, protect the relationships God has woven into your story.

Strong relationships often serve as a safeguard in seasons of testing. When the storms of life come, it is usually through the counsel, prayers, and encouragement of others that God reminds us of His promises and strengthens our faith to hold on. Protecting and nurturing these divine connections is therefore not optional.

Sustaining Your Miracle Through Covenant with God

Think of a river: as long as it stays connected to its source, it flows strong. Cut it off, and it dries up. Miracles function in the same way. They are not meant to exist apart from God's presence. When we step away from Him, through disobedience, neglect, or unbelief, we lose the life and sustenance that keep His blessings alive.

The story of Israel in the wilderness illustrates this vividly. God delivered His people from Egypt with astonishing signs and wonders. He parted the Red Sea, sent manna from heaven, and guided them by a pillar of cloud and fire. Yet, even after all those miracles, they grumbled, rebelled, and refused to trust Him.

Their broken covenant delayed their inheritance, and instead of entering the Promised Land quickly, they wandered in the wilderness for forty years. In the end, only their children walked into the promise. Their story reminds us that miracles are not lost because God changes His mind, but because His people disconnected from the atmosphere where miracles are meant to thrive. To sustain miracles, we must remain in covenant with God.

King David understood this principle well. Before every battle, he sought God's direction rather than assuming he knew what to do. Jesus modeled the same posture of dependence, living in constant communion with the Father so that each miracle flowed in perfect timing.

Ultimately, sustaining a miracle is not about formulas but about intimacy. Jesus put it plainly: *"I am the vine; you are the branches. If you remain in me and I in you, you will bear much fruit; apart from me you can do nothing"* (John 15:5). A fish removed from water doesn't die because the water lost its power, but because it was separated from its source. In the same way, miracles fade when we disconnect from God.

This is why revivals, whether in a person, a church, or even a nation, can burn brightly for a season and then fade. The change does not come from God withdrawing His blessing, but from people drifting away from abiding in Him. Keeping a miracle alive is not a one-time act but a lifelong journey of covenant where we choose to remain close to God with intentionality, perseverance, and commitment. When we do, His blessings, provision, and supernatural power continue to flow unhindered in our lives.

Key Principles to Keep Miracles Alive

Keeping a miracle alive calls for intentional stewardship. Here are key principles that help sustain the blessings and breakthroughs He has entrusted to you:

- *Stay Intentional:* Guard your miracle with the same focus and faith you used to receive it. Miracles are not passive gifts; they are entrusted blessings to be stewarded with care.
- *Maintain Relationships:* Honor the people God used to deliver your blessing. Neglecting divine connections can weaken the foundation of your miracle.
- *Stay in Covenant:* Keep nurturing your relationship with God through prayer, obedience, and intimacy. Remaining connected to the Source ensures the flow of His power.

- *Combat Spiritual Attack:* The enemy seeks to steal what God has given (John 10:10). Stay vigilant, anchored in the Word, and clothed in God's armor so you can resist his schemes.

- *Commit to Lifelong Faith:* Miracles thrive in an atmosphere of sustained belief. Keep walking in trust, dependence, and daily alignment with God's presence.

Miracles are not lost because God changes His mind; they are lost when we disconnect from the atmosphere in which they were meant to thrive. Like a fish out of water, a miracle cannot survive when separated from its source. Sustaining the miraculous is not a one-time act but a lifelong journey of faith, obedience, and intentionality.

THOUGHTS FOR REFLECTION

1. What miracle has God entrusted to you that you need to guard and sustain with renewed intentionality?
2. Are there relationships God used to bless you that you may have neglected or taken for granted? How can you honor them today?
3. In what ways are you actively nurturing your covenant relationship with God?
4. Where have you noticed the enemy trying to steal, weaken, or distract you from the miracle God gave you?
5. How can you cultivate a faith that is not just for a moment but for a lifetime?

PUT IT INTO PRACTICE

Take one intentional step to protect a miracle God has given you. This could mean deepening your relationship with God through prayer and intimacy, or reconnecting with a mentor or spiritual leader He once used to bless you but that you may have neglected.

Remember, miracles are not just received; they are stewarded, and God has entrusted you to keep them alive through faith, obedience, and daily dependence on Him.

Part Four
Witnesses of the Miraculous

Miracles are never meant to remain hidden. Throughout Scripture and history, God has worked wonders that left behind witnesses, men and women whose lives carried the undeniable mark of His power. Their stories were told so others could see, believe, and hope again.

In this section, you will encounter testimonies from my own family and from others whose lives were touched by God's intervention. From Miracle's birth to the stories of my other daughters, and from present-day believers who have experienced His hand, these accounts reveal how God continues to make Himself known through extraordinary acts in ordinary lives.

Each testimony stands as a reminder that God's power is not confined to the pages of the past. He is still moving, still healing, still providing, and still writing stories that declare His glory through those who dare to believe.

12

Miracle's Journey: From Promise to Manifestation

Every miracle follows a journey, a divine path that begins with God's promise and culminates in its visible manifestation. Understanding this journey helps us discern God's timing, respond in faith, and participate actively in what He is doing. A miracle does not simply appear out of nowhere. It unfolds in stages, each requiring patience, obedience, and alignment with God's will.

This journey often includes several key phases: the reception of a promise, the cultivation of faith, spiritual preparation, divine timing, and ultimate fulfillment. Just as a seed must be planted, nurtured, and protected before it grows into a flourishing plant, the promise of a miracle demands consistent trust, care, and cooperation with the Spirit of God until it becomes reality.

Throughout this book, I have shared glimpses of our

daughter Miracle's story. In this chapter, I want to give the full picture of how God transformed His promise into a living testimony.

The Dream and the Name

My wife, Elsie, was pregnant with our first child, and almost every day she asked what name we would give the baby. At first, I brushed it off. "I don't even know if it's a boy or a girl," I told her. "Let me pray about it and see what comes to me." Still, she pressed for an answer. Being a typical man, I thought to myself, *"I have nine months to figure this out."*

One night, I went to bed and had a dream. In the dream, I saw a beautiful little girl standing in front of the garage of our house. I called to her, "Miracle, come, come to your dad." At the time, I did not fully understand the weight of that name, but I knew in my spirit it was a seed God was planting.

When I woke up, I shook my wife and said, "I just had a dream. I don't know if the baby will be a boy or a girl, but if it's a girl, her name will be Miracle."

As soon as she heard the name, Elsie sat up, visibly upset.

"What kind of name is that? Miracle?!" she exclaimed.

I simply shrugged. "I can't fully explain it, but that's the name I heard in my dream. If it's a girl, her name will be Miracle."

She continued to suggest trendy names, but I remained firm. "If it's a girl, her name will be Miracle."

The First Challenge

During the first trimester checkup, the doctor delivered devastating news. "Mr. and Mrs. Otoo," he said, "I'm afraid I don't have good news. The sonogram shows a problem with your cervix. There's a small hole. This means your cervix is incompetent, and it could begin to dilate before the pregnancy reaches full term, putting the baby at serious risk."

Neither of us fully understood the medical terminology, but we felt the weight of his words immediately. The doctor explained that a procedure called a cerclage, which involves stitching the cervix closed, could help keep the pregnancy safe. Without it, the risk of miscarriage was high.

The procedure was performed and at first seemed successful. But soon after, Elsie began bleeding. The cervix had opened again, and the amniotic sac had begun to protrude. We rushed back to the hospital and were referred to a leading specialist.

She explained the situation was extremely complicated. The first procedure had failed, and now the baby would need to be pushed back into the womb before another stitch could be attempted. The process carried three enormous challenges.

First, the amniotic sac—the thin, delicate membrane holding the baby—had to be pushed back without breaking. To do this, a needle would remove some fluid to create space. But the pressure had to be exact: too little, and the sac would not move; too much, and it could rupture, ending the pregnancy.

Second, the needle had to avoid the four-month-old fetus, who was constantly moving. A single accidental poke could cause lifelong complications, yet the doctors had no way to predict the baby's movements.

Third, even if the sac was repositioned, the cervix still had to be stitched shut, something that would only be possible if enough tissue remained to hold the stitches.

Our child's survival depended on all three obstacles being overcome. The specialist admitted she had never attempted this procedure. At that moment, we knew only a miracle could save her.

Prayer as a Bridge

The procedure was scheduled for Monday. That weekend, I prayed with intensity, asking God to guide the doctors' hands and preserve our baby's life. After surgery, the specialist returned in amazement. "This is incredible," she said. "I've never had such a technically complicated procedure feel so straightforward. It was one of the easiest I've ever done."

That's the power of prayer. It bridges human effort with divine intervention and creates room for God to move beyond what is medically or humanly possible.

But the challenges were not over. After the second procedure, the cervix tore again and bleeding became a daily reality. The medical team advised us to consider terminating the pregnancy for Elsie's safety. Yet we chose to wait and trust God. It was not an easy decision. We knew the risks, but we clung to the word God had given us.

One exhausting day, after yet another wave of discouraging reports, Elsie broke down and said, "You know what? If this child is really born, it will be a miracle." At that point, she was at her lowest. She added, "This child, we will have to call her Wonder, or Miracle, or something." I reminded her of the dream then, and together we accepted it. Soon after, we found out the baby was a girl.

Miracle Is Born

At 24 weeks, Miracle was born. She weighed 1 pound and 9 ounces, the smallest baby I had ever seen. She could fit right in the palm of my hand. Immediately after birth, she was taken to the neonatal intensive care unit (NICU), surrounded by tubes and monitors. The doctors warned us that she would likely be blind, deaf, lame, mentally impaired, or face severe developmental challenges. But none of those things happened.

In that moment, I took it upon myself to speak life over her. Every negative word from the doctors was met with declarations of God's promises. I prayed, "In the name of Jesus, you will live and not die. You will not be blind, deaf, lame, or face developmental issues. You will be perfect because you are a gift from God."

I reassured her daily: "Don't worry. Jesus will help you. Jesus will heal you. He will take care of you. You will grow in wisdom and stature, and you will have favor with God and with man." Even at that fragile stage, I believed she could sense and respond to the words spoken over her.

The NICU Journey

The NICU became our second home. The days and weeks that followed were the most challenging of our lives. It was heartbreaking to see Miracle struggle, knowing we had no power of our own to save her.

We faced setbacks that could have shaken even the strongest faith. Some nights we did not know if she would survive until morning. I remember watching her tiny chest rise and fall with labored breaths, never taking a single moment for granted.

Through it all, we held on to the name God had given us: *Miracle*. It became our battle cry. In every prayer, we spoke life over her. We surrounded her with declarations of healing. We reminded ourselves that God had begun this story and that He would be faithful to complete it.

Elsie and I spent every possible moment by her side, praying, and offering love and comfort. Simple acts—holding her tiny hand, whispering words of encouragement, gently touching her skin—became expressions of faith that strengthened her and us.

We also encouraged other families in the NICU, sharing prayers and hope. One father, whose baby was in worse condition than Miracle, renewed his faith and presence. I believe it positively impacted his child's survival.

Day by day, breath by breath, Miracle gained strength. And slowly, the impossible began to look possible. After three months, we finally brought her home, still attached to a monitor to track her vitals. Every follow-up test showed clear results. Her vision and hearing were perfect, and she met every developmental milestone on time. She could speak, learn, and thrive, proving again that God's hand was upon her.

The Power of Faith and Words

This journey taught us the difference between facts and truth. Doctors provided facts based on evidence, but God spoke truth that surpassed human understanding.

God created the world by speaking it into existence. This reveals how powerful words are. In the same way, when doctors, who are authorities in their field, speak a prognosis, their words carry weight and influence. Proverbs 18:21 (NKJV) says, *"Death and life are in the power of the tongue."*

I did not argue with the doctors or disrespect them, but I knew I had to exercise my authority as a father and a believer. By speaking life, faith, and promises over Miracle, we aligned ourselves with God's truth rather than fear.

The NICU experience also showed us that miracles often unfold over time. Faith is not the absence of fear but the choice to trust God beyond the circumstances. Every breath, every gram gained, every milestone celebrated was a testament to His faithfulness.

Extending the Miracle

Not long after, a pastor friend of mine had a critically premature baby. I walked him through the same strategies of prayer and faith we had employed, teaching him how to pray and sharing the declarations I had spoken over Miracle.

His baby was even smaller than she had been, yet through faith and prayer, that child also survived and thrived. Miracle's story became a symbol of hope, not just for our family but for others as well.

Miracle Today

Today Miracle is a joyful, energetic young woman, and a living testimony of God's power and faithfulness. Every day, she reminds us that God's promises are *yes and amen.*

Her journey shows us that miracles are rarely instantaneous. They often require patience, perseverance, and speaking life even when circumstances seem impossible. Through her story, we learned that God works through faith, prayer, and persistence. What He begins, He is faithful to complete. When I look at Miracle, I don't just see my daughter. I see the faithfulness of the God who kept her alive when there was no medical reason for her to survive.

This journey taught us that miracles are not always sudden. Sometimes they unfold slowly, requiring us to trust God in the waiting. It showed us that faith is not the absence of fear but the decision to believe that God is greater than our fears. Even in the darkest moments, His light still shines.

As I share this story, I want you to know that what God did for us, He can do for you. Your situation may be different, but His power is the same. The God who sustained Miracle can sustain you. The God who turned our impossible situation into a testimony of life can do the same for you.

Let Miracle's story be a declaration of hope. Let it remind you that God is still writing stories of redemption, healing, and restoration. No matter how dire the diagnosis, how empty the bank account, or how broken the heart, He is still the God of miracles.

My prayer is that this chapter encourages you to believe again, to hold fast to the promises He has spoken over your life, to trust that even when you cannot see the way forward, He is working beyond what you can imagine. And remember always: what He begins, He is faithful to complete.

Looking back, I see that Miracle's journey was God's way of preparing our faith for the seasons ahead, especially for the pregnancies and births of her three sisters, each of which brought its own lessons in trust and surrender.

13

My Other Daughters' Stories: More Miracles to Tell

Every child's story is unique, yet each one reflects the hand of God in a different way. After walking through Miracle's journey, I thought I had already seen the fullness of His wonder. But He wasn't finished. With each of my other daughters, He revealed another side of His miraculous power.

These stories go beyond the extraordinary. They illustrate the principles of faith, prayer, obedience, and divine timing in real life. Each reveals that miracles are not reserved for a select few but are available to all who trust, persevere, and walk with Him.

As you read my daughters' testimonies, allow these testimonies to strengthen your faith, stir fresh expectancy, and deepen your understanding of how the miraculous moves in ordinary lives. Here, the supernatural becomes tangible and the invisible power of God is made visible through the experiences of those who dared to believe.

Christina's Story

The pregnancy with Miracle and everything we went through was so traumatic that Elsie and I even wondered if we would be able to have other children. We prayed, yet the pressure and uncertainty remained.

Sometime later, we found out she was pregnant again. At our first check-up, the tests revealed her hCG hormone level was very low, around 150. This hormone is crucial because it signals that the pregnancy is developing normally. The nurse, seeing the number, immediately asked if we were there for a Dilation and Curettage (D&C), a procedure typically used after a miscarriage or for an abortion, assuming that such a low level meant the pregnancy was no longer viable.

It was a shock for us, especially since we had just found out we were pregnant and had come for a routine visit. Because this was the same hospital where Miracle had been born, some of the staff already knew us. They informed us that, given our history, it was highly likely that this pregnancy would either be ectopic (outside the uterus) or end in a miscarriage.

I simply replied to the nurse, "Thank you," then turned to Elsie and said, "I reject this pronouncement in the name of Jesus." The doctor asked us to come back later to check for any changes. She explained that if the hormone levels remained the same by the next visit, it would likely mean the pregnancy would not continue. Despite this unexpected diagnosis, we chose to trust in God and stand firm in our faith, believing that He would intervene just as He had with Miracle.

We went home and prayed. At our next visit, the hormone level had risen to 200. Unfortunately, that still wasn't high enough, so the doctor gave us another three days to monitor the situation. By then, it had jumped to 1,500. Even with that increase, the doctor remained cautious and warned us of potential complications. Realizing the need for a supportive environment, we decided to transfer to a different hospital.

If you are expecting a miracle, remember that the environment around you matters. At times, you may need to make a change, whether that means switching hospitals, seeking new counsel, or stepping away from places that do not align with your faith and expectations. Surround yourself with people who will believe with you and create an atmosphere of support and trust in God's power. Faith flourishes in the right environment, and that can make all the difference in seeing your miracle come to pass. Trust that God will lead you to the place where His will can be fully manifested.

So we transferred to a different hospital. The new doctor required weekly check-ups for the rest of the pregnancy. It was a challenging season. Miracle was still a toddler, and we spent week after week at appointments. Elsie couldn't travel or do much, so our lives had to adjust around this pregnancy and the care it required.

Unlike her first pregnancy, she faced no issues with an incompetent cervix this time. The doctor was so surprised she even suggested doing a preventive procedure anyway. But we refused. We told her, "If there's no problem, let's leave it alone." So up until it was time to deliver Christina, my wife's cervix remained intact.

While Miracle was born prematurely, Christina was born two weeks past full term, at 42 weeks. Her delivery was very difficult, and Elsie suffered significant tearing. Even weeks afterward, she was in pain and had trouble sitting or moving. Despite those challenges, we knew God's hand was on us and trusted He would carry us through this journey with Christina, just as He had before.

Zoey's Story

Zoey's pregnancy battled normally, though Elsie struggled with persistent nausea. At first, it seemed like the usual discomfort of early pregnancy, but as the weeks passed, it became clear this was no ordinary morning sickness.

At one appointment, she was diagnosed with hyperemesis gravidarum, which is a severe condition that causes relentless nausea and makes eating nearly impossible. Instead of gaining weight, she was losing it, which is always worrying in pregnancy.

By the fifth month, things took a terrifying turn. One day, she began bleeding. It wasn't just spotting; it was enough to make my heart sink. We rushed to the hospital, and I held her hand the whole way, praying silently. When the doctor examined her, the news was worse than we imagined: the placenta had partially detached from the uterine wall.

This condition, called placental abruption, meant the baby was not receiving enough oxygen and nutrients to grow. The doctor's expression was grave as he explained the danger. "This isn't just about the bleeding," he said. "The baby is in real danger."

Elsie was already struggling to eat or keep anything down because of hyperemesis, and now her body could no longer fully sustain the pregnancy. Without proper nourishment, the baby's growth would be compromised. The body would prioritize the most vital organs, like the brain, leaving other parts, such as the arms or legs, underdeveloped. "There's a strong chance the baby could be born with deformities," the doctor warned.

His words hit us like a ton of bricks. I looked at my wife and saw the pain in her eyes. She already felt helpless, unable to eat or give our baby what she needed. The guilt weighed on both of us like a heavy cloud.

There was nothing we could do to reattach the placenta, nothing we could do to ensure the baby was getting what it needed to grow and thrive. The stress, the frustration, the helplessness, and the overall sense of complete powerlessness were crushing.

But even in the face of such bleak news, we held on to hope. We prayed fervently, asking God to step in a situation that was completely out of our hands. It wasn't easy. Every day tested our faith, but we chose to believe that God's plans were greater than the doctor's report.

And then, God showed us His power. When Zoey was born, she defied every expectation. The baby the doctors said might suffer deformities was born completely healthy. She was fully developed, with a sharp mind and strong spirit. She was perfect.

In that moment, we saw firsthand that God is the helper of the helpless. He is the One who steps in when we reach our limits. Only He can make the impossible possible.

Angela's Story

I was in the Bahamas planting a church when my wife called me with unexpected news. "I'm pregnant," she said, her voice a mix of excitement and nervousness. At first, I thought she was joking.

Our youngest, Zoey, was still a baby, and the idea of another child so soon felt almost surreal. I laughed, waiting for her to tell me it was a prank. But her voice turned serious, and I knew this was real. The news made us happy, but it also brought worry. Her first three pregnancies had been incredibly difficult. Would this one be just as hard, or worse?

It didn't take long to find out. Within weeks, the familiar pattern returned. She couldn't keep anything down—no food, no water, not even a sip of juice. The nausea was relentless. Some days, it was so severe she screamed in pain, as though something were tearing her apart inside. Other days, she passed out from sheer exhaustion. It was heartbreaking to watch her suffer.

Day after day, she grew thinner and weaker. By her third trimester, she had lost over 80 pounds. It was terrifying. I couldn't help but wonder how her weak body could keep going, let alone carry a baby to term.

Yet even in her weakness, her spirit remained strong. We continually turned to God in prayer, crying out for strength, healing, and mercy. There were times I wondered if we would make it through. Watching the woman I loved suffer like that was one of the most painful experiences of my life. And yet, she endured. Even when her body was failing, her spirit held on. Her quiet strength amazed me. Somehow, even at her absolute weakest, she kept going.

When the day of delivery finally came, though Elsie was drained, she brought the baby safely into the world.
Holding that baby in my arms, I felt overwhelmed with gratitude and awe. That moment reminded us of God's faithfulness. In every struggle, every prayer, and every sleepless night, He was present. He carried us when we could not carry ourselves. He gave us strength when we had none and brought us through a storm we thought might break us.

These stories are more than family history. They are living testimonies of God's miraculous power. Each child's journey shows how faith, persistent prayer, trust in God's timing, and reliance on His protection can transform impossible circumstances into extraordinary miracles. Christina, Zoey, and Angela remind us that God is still at work, orchestrating wonders for those who believe, trust, and remain faithful.

Our story is not the only testimony of God's miraculous power. Over the years, we have seen Him move not only in our family but in the lives of countless others. As a bishop and a witness to His goodness, I have seen God's faithfulness repeated again and again.

In the next chapter, I want to share some of those incredible testimonies with you. My prayer is that as you read them, your faith will be encouraged and you will be reminded that God is still working miracles today.

14

Testimonies of God's Miracles Today

Hebrews 12:1 speaks of a "great cloud of witnesses," reminding us that throughout history, men and women have testified to God's power and faithfulness. That witness continues today. The testimonies in this chapter are living evidence that the God who performed miracles in Scripture is still intervening in ways that defy human explanation.

These stories come from ordinary people whose lives were transformed by extraordinary encounters with God. They stand as present-day witnesses to His faithfulness and invite you to believe that what He has done before, He can do again.

For the sake of privacy, some names and identifying details have been changed.

From Stillbirth to Miracle Baby - Tina

My husband and I got married in September 2015, and by March 2016, we found out I was pregnant. Everything seemed fine with the pregnancy until, during a routine visit in the fifth month, we discovered that the baby was not developing well. We were instructed to go to the hospital immediately, where we were faced with our worst nightmare: we were told to terminate the pregnancy. But because the baby still had a heartbeat, we chose to continue the pregnancy.

The doctors told us there was nothing they could do to save the child and advised us to go home and wait for the bleeding to start.

In the seventh month, the baby passed away in my womb. The doctor confirmed that the heartbeat had stopped, and after eighteen hours of labor, I delivered our stillborn baby boy. That day, we left all memories of the baby we had named Strength at the hospital.

Thus began four years of intense emotional pain as we struggled to conceive again. During this time, we placed the crib that had belonged to Bishop Dr. Kibby's daughter, Miracle, in our bedroom and used it as a point of contact, praying that the same God who blessed his daughter, Miracle, would bless us as well.

In September 2020, I came home from work, and my husband told me that Bishop Kibby wanted me to call him. When I did, he shared that he had been praying with the church's intercessor team and he felt strongly that our breakthrough was on its way. He spoke with such certainty and ended the call with an overwhelming sense of faith and assurance that good news was on the way.

About two weeks later, I started feeling a little different than usual and noticed my menstrual cycle was about three days late. I told my husband that we should take a pregnancy test. After taking so many tests in the past that had all come back negative, he had said no more. I was extremely nervous and didn't want to face another disappointment. I peed in a cup, quickly handed it to him, and ran to hide in the kitchen while he completed the test.

When I heard him close the door, I felt terrible, assuming the result was negative. He wouldn't open the door until I knocked repeatedly. Finally, when he opened it, he showed me the result. It was positive! I screamed, fell to the floor, and thanked God through tears of joy. We immediately called Bishop Kibby, who was overjoyed but not surprised, reminding us of his call from two weeks earlier.

Bishop Kibby was with us every step of the way, from conception to delivery. He prayed with us day and night, gave us directions, and stayed in constant contact. He even came to my work every week to check on the baby and me, praying with us each time. He supported and prayed us through every appointment, and on multiple occasions, he challenged the doctors and changed their recommendations.

On delivery day, he drove two hours at midnight to be there and was the first to see baby D.D.B. God used Bishop Dr. Kibby Otoo strategically as a spiritual midwife to prophesy our child and pray us through the pregnancy until our miracle baby was born. We give all glory and honor to God for His faithfulness and for blessing us with such a wonderful father in our Bishop, who helped bring forth this miracle. Thank you, God, and may God richly bless you, Daddy Bishop!

From Being Called Sterile to Becoming a Joyful Mother - Mary

When my husband and I got married, having children wasn't part of our immediate plan. We wanted to enjoy our new marriage as much as possible, though we weren't actively trying to prevent a pregnancy either.

After a year passed, we began thinking more seriously about starting a family. We tried naturally for several months, but nothing happened. I started seeing a gynecologist to rule out any issues and she advised to begin with the least invasive tests. One by one, the results came back normal, and the doctor couldn't determine what the problem was.

Several months into testing and more than two years into our marriage, the doctor finally recommended the most invasive procedure, a hysterosalpingography, to definitively rule out any fertility issues.

A hysterosalpingography, or HSG, is a test in which dye is injected into the fallopian tubes to check for blockages that might prevent conception. For some reason, I found myself hesitating. I finally decided to wait a few more months to see if a pregnancy would happen naturally. Sadly, nothing changed.

Finally, in January 2021, as we entered our third year of marriage, I realized something had to shift. I had grown tired of waiting and scheduled the HSG. But just a couple of days before the appointment, as I prayed about it, I felt a strong lack of peace that I couldn't ignore. I told the Lord, "Okay, I won't go," and in that moment, I felt His peace wash over me like a comforting wave.

I decided to trust the Lord with the situation and canceled the test. Throughout that time, He continued to remind me of His promises: that He is the one who opens the womb, and of a specific dream He had given me in which I saw myself taking a pregnancy test that came back positive. Still, as more months passed, nothing happened.

By May 2021, I was feeling deeply discouraged and decided to schedule the HSG test after all. During prayer, I told the Lord that I couldn't keep going without understanding what was happening with my body. I didn't hear anything back. Or perhaps I was too stubborn to recognize His voice. So on May 5, 2021, I went to the hospital for the test.

It turned out to be one of the most painful experiences I had ever endured, physically and emotionally. As the dye was inserted, I could see from the screen that it wasn't flowing through the fallopian tubes. The technician informed me that it appeared both tubes were blocked, but the final word would come from the doctor. Several hours later, the doctor called to confirm the results and offered to refer me to fertility specialists to explore the possibility of pregnancy through in-vitro fertilization (IVF).

Still in shock, I called my husband to share the news, but he didn't seem to grasp the full weight of what I was feeling. It felt like my world was crashing down. But even in my pain, I refused to accept the finality of the diagnosis. I printed the test results and brought them to church with me. I didn't even tell Bishop Kibby. After everyone had left the sanctuary, I quietly walked to the pulpit, placed the paper beneath it, and told God, "This is Your business now. I will not receive the children You promised me through IVF." With complete honesty, I said, "Lord, I have seen You move in this house and on this altar. You will need to take care of this because I simply cannot."

Several months earlier, the Lord had used one of His servants to speak a word over me, declaring that He would show His power in my life and that no one could stop His will for me to have the children He had promised. The servant went further, saying that between May and June 2021, I would witness God's glory.

So when May 2021 arrived, and I received the painful results from my HSG test, I clung to the little faith I had left. May came and went without any sign of change. As June began, I watched each day pass with quiet anticipation, wondering if and how God would move, especially since the end of June also marked the end of my menstrual cycle.

June 30, 2021, the last day of the month, finally arrived, and I couldn't sit still. I went to work, but I couldn't concentrate on anything. As soon as the workday ended, I decided to take a pregnancy test. I had taken so many before, all of them negative, so I was hesitant and anxious to face another possible disappointment. But this time felt different. I had received such a specific word from the Lord, that He would do it for me between May and June, and now I had reached the final day for the manifestation of that promise.

So, I took the test. I was so nervous I couldn't even bring myself to look at the stick while waiting for the result to appear. I left it in the bathroom, set a timer, and went to my room, quietly calling on the name of Jesus. When the timer went off, I rushed back into the bathroom. The test was positive. I dropped to my knees, overwhelmed, sobbing, and all I could do was cry out, "Jesus! Jesus! Jesus!"

My pregnancy progressed smoothly and without complications, something I did not take for granted. I knew Bishop Kibby and the team of intercessors he had dispatched were faithfully praying for me and the baby.

In early 2022, I gave birth to a healthy baby boy, to the glory of the Lord! Truly, God still works miracles. The one who had once been labeled barren by medical science was now, in the words of Psalm 113:9, *"a joyous mother of children."*

I give all the glory to God, and my husband, my children, and I are eternally grateful to Bishop Kibby for his love, sacrifice, and unceasing prayers.

Saved from Miscarriage - Tanya

When I became pregnant, I didn't know it at first. Then, suddenly, I started bleeding, so I went to the hospital to find out what was happening. That's when I learned I was pregnant. The HCG levels that indicate a healthy pregnancy are usually in the thousands, but mine was only around 1,000. Since I was still bleeding, I returned for another test. This time, the levels had dropped into the double digits. The doctor gently told me, sadly, that there was nothing they could do and advised me to relax, as my body would eventually let the baby go on its own.

But I refused to accept that outcome. I declared that as a child of God, I would not lose my baby. The Word of God says, *"You will serve the Lord, and none shall miscarry."* I held on to that promise and refused to miscarry my baby. When the doctor delivered the news, I said, *"God forbid"* in my heart, immediately rejecting the negative report. I politely thanked the doctor and walked out.

I thank God for my husband, too. He was a great support during that time. While I expected him to hug me and grieve with me over the sad news, instead, he said firmly, "No, the devil cannot do this." His words strengthened my faith. In that moment, I chose to hold on to one truth: this was not from God. I believed that God would not take away a gift He had given. Though I had moments of sadness, I continued to worship and trust in His faithfulness.

During this time, my husband and I decided that I would

keep attending church, even though I was technically supposed to be on bed rest. I remember one particular service where I sat in worship, tears streaming down my face as I felt the bleeding continue. Even in that moment, I made a conscious decision not to dwell on the bleeding and not to give the devil any glory.

I remember one church service when Bishop Kibby called me up. He had me sit down, placed his hands on my shoulders, and prayed for me. My husband joined in, praying, too, and together, they lifted me up in prayer. Then, Bishop Kibby told me to go lie down on the altar.

As I lay there, I cried out to God, "Lord, I know that my good deeds are like filthy rags before You, but today, let my service in this house speak for me. The God of Bishop Kibby and Lady Elsie, who bled for six months and did not lose her baby, will not allow me to lose mine. This will not be my testimony in this house." I continued to pray fervently.

Then, suddenly, I felt something strike my stomach, even though the lights were off and no one was near. I began to tremble and asked God, "What is this?"

After the prayer, I got up and thanked God, unsure of what had happened. Before that day, the doctors had suggested an ultrasound but later decided it wasn't necessary, insisting there would be nothing to see. They believed that by then, the pregnancy would have resolved on its own and the baby would have already been evacuated from my body.

The following month, I decided to visit the doctor again. To my amazement, the doctor asked why I had never gone for the ultrasound, then revealed that the baby was, in fact, growing in my womb. I was stunned, as I had been told I was losing my baby. The doctor confirmed it again: the baby was growing.

Seven months later, I gave birth to a healthy baby, to the glory of God. I am so grateful, and all I can say is, "*Hallelujah!*"

A Miraculous Pregnancy Against All Odds - Faith

I am deeply grateful to the Lord for my child. Time and again, doctors and others declared that it would not be possible for me to give birth, but the Lord proved everyone wrong. At one point, my husband and I visited one of the largest hospitals in the region, where the doctors said that my body was actually fighting the pregnancy.

Through it all, Bishop Kibby stood in the gap. He continually boosted our faith, speaking life when the reports spoke death. Every time a negative diagnosis came in, he would declare the opposite, and his words gave us the strength to keep believing. The doctors eventually told us that we had two options: either I wouldn't make it through the pregnancy, or I would need a C-section.

When it came time to give birth, everything went smoothly, despite the complications we had prepared ourselves for. We were even chatting and laughing with the doctor when I suddenly felt something between my legs. I told her to check because I was sure the baby was coming. She initially disagreed, saying that the baby couldn't come out without any pushing. But when she finally checked, sure enough, the baby was already out!

At that very moment, the same grace that was with us moved to the room next door. A man came running out, announcing that their baby had just been born as well. It was truly the grace of God that brought us through.

Soon after, the very people who had doubted and thought they had put a stop to my life began calling, asking for pictures of me pregnant or other proof that I had really given birth because they couldn't believe it. The testimony was so mind-blowing that it didn't even make sense to me.

When people ask me about the childbirth experience, my

only response is, "God took care of it." I had prayed, "Lord, I don't want a hard labor. I want it to be easy." And God answered that prayer in full, showing Himself faithful. I am truly and deeply thankful to Him.

A Miracle Baby After Surviving an Ectopic Pregnancy - Brenda

My testimony begins in 2021, shortly after the birth of my first daughter. At the time, she was about three to four months old. Like many new mothers, I assumed the bleeding I was experiencing was just part of the normal postpartum recovery. What I didn't realize was that I was in a critical condition. I was literally dying.

Around that time, I had a dream where I felt like my body was being placed into a ditch, as if someone was laying me in a grave. Thankfully, I was connected to our church community and reached out to the pastors. I called Bishop Kibby, and as many of you know, when you speak to him, he gives clear and immediate direction. I followed his instructions carefully.

Even though the bleeding continued, I still believed it was part of the normal process. Then one Sunday morning, I woke up with my stomach bloated and visibly enlarged. I turned to my husband and said, "Instead of going to church today, please take me to the ER."

When I arrived at the ER, I expected them to tell me it was something minor. However, once the ER doctor asked about my symptoms and sent me for an ultrasound, I realized something was seriously wrong. The ultrasound technician went silent, and I immediately knew something was wrong. When I was sent back to my room, doctors began rushing in with worried expressions on their faces.

They explained that I was pregnant, but the pregnancy was ectopic and had ruptured. What shocked them the most was that I had even made it to the hospital in that condition. They kept asking, "How did you get here?" I told them my husband had dropped me off and was home with our daughter. The doctors were stunned, saying that based on the amount of blood I had lost, it didn't make sense that I was still conscious, let alone able to walk in on my own.

I was rushed into emergency surgery, where I underwent a blood transfusion and several other procedures. After the operation, there was uncertainty about whether I would ever be able to conceive again.

Later that same year, during a regular Wednesday Bible study service, Bishop Kibby looked at me and said, "God just gave you a miracle." I held on to that word with everything in me.

A few months later, I found out I was pregnant with our second daughter, who is now six months old. Every time I look at her face, it's a reminder of God's goodness. She is a living testimony that God still performs miracles.

Miraculously Healed from Life-Threatening Seizures - Amy

Sometime in 2011, my daughters went to spend the weekend with their father. That weekend, I didn't cover them in prayer as I usually did. I had gone out with friends and, in hindsight, let my guard down. When they returned, I noticed my younger daughter was acting strangely. I asked if she was feeling unwell, but she didn't respond.

The next morning, before they left for school, I prayed over both of my daughters and covered them in the blood of Jesus. All day, I kept praying. Their routine was to go from school to after-school activities at the YMCA. But while I was at work, I received a devastating call: my younger daughter had had a seizure. She fainted, was foaming at the mouth, and wasn't breathing.

I worked only 30 minutes away, but the drive felt like a lifetime. It was the worst day of my life. I called my pastors, and they met us at the hospital. They prayed over her, and by God's grace, she recovered and felt better. I thought the nightmare was over, but it wasn't.

Once we returned home, the seizures started again. The doctors did everything they could to find the cause but found no explanation. She began having seizures back-to-back. The neurologist changed her medication several times, but nothing seemed to work.

To make matters worse, my daughter was being bullied at school because of her condition. I contacted the board of directors and proposed that the school educate both students and parents about epilepsy. They agreed. With the help of her neurologist, we created a lesson plan with pictures. I went to the school and taught my daughter's peers about epilepsy, explaining what to watch for. When I asked who would be willing to help her at school, every child raised their hand. I told them, "If you see her eyes start to glaze over, tell the teacher right away." And we continued to cover her in prayer.

On May 1st of that same year, we went to my mother's house for her birthday. That day, my daughter had about 36 seizures in a row. Bishop Kibby and the church's pastors prayed around the clock. Eventually, the seizures subsided, and we were able to return home. But the next day, she had another seizure and stopped breathing.

The medics arrived and were preparing to declare her dead, but I refused to accept it. "No way," I said. I called my pastors, placed the phone on speaker, and they began to pray with authority. We prayed until she came back to life.

On another occasion, my two daughters were brushing their teeth together when my older daughter suddenly screamed. I ran into the bathroom and saw my younger daughter lying on the floor with blood everywhere. She had collapsed during a seizure and hit her head hard on the tile. She didn't even cry. She was in shock. We rushed her to the hospital for evaluation, and by God's grace, she was released the next day.

Despite everything, the medications still weren't working. The neurologist was baffled. Meanwhile, Bishop Kibby and the pastors continued to encourage me, declaring that God would heal her. But instead of getting better, things got worse. They kept praying, standing in the gap, refusing to back down.

The final set of medications the neurologist gave her caused alarming side effects. She began to fall while walking, her hands stopped functioning properly, and her speech became slurred. At that point, Bishop Kibby called for a three-day fast specifically for my daughter. We prayed day and night, refusing to give up the fight.

After that time of fasting and prayer, God had mercy upon us and answered our prayers. My daughter was miraculously healed! Today, you can't stop her from talking. She's full of life and now thriving in college by God's grace. She's the same child some teachers had once written off. But God had the final word.

We give God all the glory. I am so grateful for Bishop Kibby, my pastors and above all, a praying church.

Part Five
Walking in Miracles Today

Miracles are not sealed in the past. They are alive, active, and accessible to every believer in this generation. They are not meant to be rare or occasional but a lifestyle and an ongoing testimony that *"the Kingdom of God has come near"* (Luke 10:9).

The miraculous is evidence of God's Kingdom breaking into the ordinary. Signs and wonders are not the goal. Rather, they are the fruit of intimacy with the Miracle-Worker, the overflow of a life yielded to the Spirit, and the mark of His presence at work among His people.

In this section, we will see how miracles manifest not only in great crusades or dramatic events, but also in the hidden corners of our daily lives, in the mission of the Church, and in the believer's personal walk with God. From quiet provisions to dramatic interventions, miracles are God's way of weaving eternity into time.

The story of miracles did not end with the book of Acts. It continues, in you and with you.

15

Everyday Miracles

The miraculous is not always spectacular; sometimes it is subtle. Some of God's greatest works come quietly, clothed in simplicity, almost hidden in the fabric of daily life, such as a whisper of grace, a door opened at the right moment, or a provision that arrives when no one knew of the need.

The God who parts seas and raises the dead is also the God of daily bread. His power is not limited to dramatic events or public displays; it is just as present in the hidden mercies that sustain us one day at a time.

In this chapter, we will explore how miracles reveal themselves in ordinary places, through provision, protection, healing, joy, peace, and divine connections. These are the wonders that remind us God is near, weaving His presence into the small details of our lives.

The God of Daily Bread

One of the clearest ways God reveals His care is through provision. In the wilderness, Israel awoke each morning to manna scattered like dew (Exodus 16:4). What sustained them was not a banquet but a simple daily provision, fresh and sufficient. God taught them to rely on Him one day at a time, showing that His presence was their true security.

Stories like these continue today. A young mother, with an empty pantry and no money to spare, whispered a prayer no one else ever heard. That same evening, a neighbor arrived unexpectedly with bags of groceries. Heaven had heard her sigh, and provision came at just the right moment.

The same God who feeds individuals also provides for entire communities. During a mission trip in Latin America, food prepared for only fifty people ended up feeding more than two hundred, with leftovers. For those who witnessed it, the miracle was not simply about bread on the table; it was a declaration that Christ cares for everyday needs. Just as He multiplied loaves and fish by the Sea of Galilee, He still multiplies resources to sustain His people in the most practical of ways.

Provision is God's fatherhood in action. It declares, "You are not forgotten. I will sustain you." Jesus taught us to pray, *"Give us this day our daily bread"* (Matthew 6:11). The miracle is not only the bread but the timing. God's provision comes with precision, arriving at the very moment of need and reminding us that He sees even the smallest details of our lives.

If you need to experience God in His provision, pray this: *Lord, open my eyes to see Your hand in daily provision. Teach me to trust You one day at a time, and to thank You for every good gift that comes from above.*

Protection in the Unseen

God's protection often surrounds us in ways we do not see or recognize. Many of His greatest miracles are the dangers we never encounter because His hand has already intervened.

When Elisha's servant trembled before the enemy's armies, Elisha prayed, and the young man's eyes were opened to see angelic hosts surrounding them (2 Kings 6:17). Victory was already secured before fear had a chance to take root. In the same way, a man once missed his usual bus and grumbled at the inconvenience, only to learn later that the very bus had been involved in a fatal crash. What seemed like delay was in fact divine rescue.

God's angels often work silently, shielding us in ways we may never fully grasp until eternity. His protection is steady, precise, and deeply personal.

If you need to experience God's protection in a deeper way, pray this: *Father, thank You for unseen victories and silent rescues. Keep me hidden beneath the shadow of Your wings.*

Divine Connections and Timely Encounters

Miracles are not always dramatic healings or signs in the sky but the right person at the right time. God weaves lives together in ways that reveal His hand guiding every step.

Ruth's story shows this clearly. While gleaning in the fields to survive, she "happened" to find herself in Boaz's field (Ruth 2:3). What looked like chance was actually divine orchestration that secured her future and tied her into God's redemptive plan. Through that connection, Ruth found not only provision but also favor, protection, and ultimately a place in the lineage of Christ.

In a similar way, a reluctant businesswoman attended a conference she almost skipped. By what seemed like random seating, she found herself beside an investor who not only believed in her vision but also provided the resources to launch it. That single encounter became the key that unlocked her calling and transformed her business.

Heaven arranges meetings that alter destinies. What we often call coincidence is really God's appointment, aligning us with people connected to our purpose. Divine connections remind us that God orders our steps, placing us in the right place at the right time for purposes greater than we could design ourselves.

If you need God to align your steps with the right people and opportunities, pray this: *Lord, order my steps into divine encounters. Align me with those connected to my purpose.*

Peace Beyond Understanding

Sometimes, the miracle is not the removal of the storm but the calm God provides in the midst of it. His peace is itself a sign of His presence.

During the storm on the Sea of Galilee, while the disciples panicked and feared for their lives, Jesus slept in peace (Mark 4:38). His calm in the chaos was not indifference but confidence in the Father's care.

That same miracle still happens today. A man who suddenly lost his job expected fear, anxiety, and sleepless nights. Instead, he found himself sustained by an overwhelming peace he could not explain. While the bills still piled up and uncertainty remained, he testified that God's peace guarded his heart until a better opportunity opened for him. The real miracle is often the peace that steadies us while the storm still rages.

The world looks for security in circumstances, but God gives peace that surpasses understanding, holding us steady when nothing else can.

If you need that kind of peace today, pray this: *Jesus, fill me with Your peace that surpasses understanding, even in life's uncertainties.*

Healing in Subtle Ways

Not every miracle happens in an instant. Some unfold slowly, almost quietly, until one day we realize the affliction is gone.

Naaman expected a dramatic display of power when he sought healing for his leprosy. Instead, Elisha told him to simply dip seven times in the Jordan River (2 Kings 5:14). At first, Naaman resisted, thinking the instructions too ordinary for such a serious condition. Yet when he obeyed, his skin was restored, proving that God's power often works through simple acts of faith.

In a similar way, a woman battling depression longed for instant deliverance. She expected one prayer to erase the struggle completely. Instead, her healing came gradually, through prayer, counseling, community support, and the slow renewal of her mind. Looking back months later, she realized freedom had dawned like the sunrise: steady, gentle, but sure.

Not every miracle is sudden. God's power is not diminished when healing takes time. Every small step of progress is still a testimony of His hand at work. Often, the process itself deepens trust and teaches perseverance.

If you need patience while waiting for breakthrough, pray this: *Father, give me patience for the process of healing. Teach me to trust that You are working even in unseen ways, and that in Your time, You will make all things new.*

Joy in the Simple Moments

Joy itself can be a miracle, especially when it blooms after a season of sorrow. God's presence has a way of turning mourning into dancing and giving laughter where tears once flowed.

Paul understood this when he urged believers to *"rejoice in the Lord always"* even while he was in prison (Philippians 4:4). His joy was not tied to comfort or freedom but to the unshakable presence of Christ. By rejoicing in chains, Paul showed that joy can flourish even in the hardest places, becoming a testimony stronger than despair.

In the same way, a grieving widower thought he would never laugh again. The weight of sorrow seemed permanent, pressing down on every part of his life. Then one afternoon, while playing with his grandchildren, he found himself laughing freely, almost surprised by the sound. That moment of joy was more than emotion; it was resurrection for his heart.

Joy after sorrow is a testimony that God restores the soul. When laughter returns, it carries the fragrance of healing and hope.

If you are longing for that kind of restoration, pray this: *Lord, restore joy where sorrow has lingered too long. Let laughter rise again.*

Testimonies of the "Little Things"

God delights in showing His presence not only in mighty acts but also in the details we might overlook. What may seem minor to us is sometimes heaven's way of saying, *"I am near."*

A student once prayed for tuition fees, and the exact amount arrived in an anonymous envelope.

A family's car broke down, and a stranger mechanic fixed it at no charge when they could not have afforded the repair.

Someone discouraged cried out for encouragement, and a friend texted the very words they needed. These are not coincidences. The same God who parts seas also pays attention to the smallest details of our lives.

If you long to notice Him in the details, pray this: *Thank You, Lord, for the quiet miracles that remind me of Your constant love.*

Living with Eyes Open

The greatest key to recognizing everyday miracles is awareness. Gratitude sharpens our vision. The more we thank God for the small, the more we begin to see His hand in all things. What others call ordinary is often heaven's extraordinary in disguise.

Everyday miracles remind us that God is not only the Lord of mountains and oceans, but also of meals, moments, and morning mercies. He is present in divine connections, daily provisions, quiet healings, and unseen protections. When we live with gratitude and expectancy, we discover that with God, nothing is ordinary; life itself is a miracle. As Proverbs 3:6 says, *"In all your ways acknowledge Him, and He shall direct your paths."*

As we close this chapter, let this prayer shape your perspective and attune your heart to God's hand in the ordinary: *Father, give me eyes that see and a heart that gives thanks, that I may never miss Your hand in my daily life. Lord, make me sensitive to Your presence in every detail. Teach me to expect Your goodness and celebrate Your miracles, both great and small.*

16

Miracles in Evangelism and Mission

From the very beginning of the Church, miracles have been inseparable from the preaching of the gospel. They are not a substitute for the Word but a confirmation of it, a divine seal upon the message of Christ.

Evangelism and mission are not merely human endeavors; they are supernatural callings that require supernatural power. As Mark records, *"They went out and preached everywhere, the Lord working with them and confirming the word through the accompanying signs"* (Mark 16:20). Wherever Christ is proclaimed, heaven bears witness. Signs do not compete with the message; they serve it, pointing hearts to the Savior.

Miracles as Divine Endorsement of the Gospel

When the apostles preached, miracles served as God's

endorsement of their message. The lame walked, the blind saw, and demons fled. These acts did not compete with the gospel; they amplified it and confirmed its truth.

In Samaria, when Philip proclaimed Christ, the crowds paid close attention because they witnessed deliverances and healings with their own eyes: *"For unclean spirits, crying with a loud voice, came out of many who had them; and many who were paralyzed or lame were healed. So there was much joy in that city"* (Acts 8:7–8). The power of God broke through spiritual bondage and physical affliction, and the result was an eager reception of the Word.

In another instance, Paul and Barnabas ministered with boldness in Iconium. As they preached, God confirmed their message by enabling them to perform signs and wonders (Acts 14:3).

Wherever the gospel was spread, heaven backed it with power. Without this witness, many might have dismissed the message as mere human philosophy, but miracles compelled attention. They were God's own signature declaring, *"This Word is from Me."*

Just as in the days of the apostles, God continues to confirm His Word through miracles that cannot be denied. One powerful account comes from India. A missionary entered a Hindu village that had resisted the gospel for decades. During his visit, he prayed for a paralyzed child, and to everyone's amazement the child rose and walked. The entire village turned to Christ as a result of that healing. He did not need to persuade the villagers with human reasoning, because they had encountered undeniable proof that Jesus is alive.

Opening Closed Doors and Resistant Hearts

Miracles not only confirm the truth of the gospel; they also break

162

through barriers that human words cannot. What convinces some people of Christ's reality is not a debate won but a wall of resistance shattered by God's power.

This is seen throughout Scripture. Cornelius, a Roman centurion, received a vision that prepared him to hear Peter's message and opened the way for the gospel to reach the Gentiles (Acts 10). Later, Paul was guided by a vision of a Macedonian man pleading for help, which redirected his journey and brought the gospel into Europe (Acts 16:9–10). These moments show how God uses supernatural encounters to open doors that would otherwise remain shut.

The same is true in our day. Missionaries serving in restricted nations often testify of people coming to Christ through dreams and visions. Such encounters cannot be manufactured or silenced. They bypass cultural and political barriers, awakening hearts that might never have listened otherwise.

When people resist the preacher, God Himself becomes the preacher. A dream can slip past guarded borders, and a healing can disarm hostility in a moment. Every culture that seems closed has a key, and often that key is the miraculous. When human words fail, divine works speak.

Demonstrating God's Compassion Alongside His Truth

Miracles in mission are never only about power; they are also about love. Jesus not only preached the kingdom but also healed the sick, fed the hungry, and delivered the oppressed. Matthew tells us that when He saw the multitudes, He was moved with compassion and healed their sick (Matthew 14:14). His compassion gave birth to miracles, and those miracles opened hearts to receive His teaching.

This truth continues wherever the gospel is proclaimed. In rural Africa, missionaries organized a medical outreach to serve impoverished families. Alongside medicine, they prayed for the sick. As malaria patients were healed instantly in the name of Jesus, hundreds came to faith. What doctors could not do, the compassion of Christ accomplished. The healings were not a show of power for its own sake but an expression of God's care that spoke more deeply than words ever could.

Power without love can become performance, but when compassion fuels miracles, they pierce hearts more effectively than sermons alone. The world does not only need proof that God exists; it also needs proof that God cares. When miracles flow from love, they reveal the heart of the Father and draw people to Him.

Signs that Confront Darkness

Every mission field is also a battlefield. When the gospel enters new territory, it often collides with spiritual powers that hold people in bondage. Miracles of deliverance reveal the superiority of Christ's kingdom over every work of darkness.

In the book of Acts, Paul encountered Elymas the sorcerer, who opposed his preaching before the proconsul of Cyprus. Paul declared God's judgment, and Elymas was struck blind. The proconsul, astonished at both the teaching and the demonstration of power, believed the gospel (Acts 13:8–12). The sign dismantled spiritual opposition and cleared the way for faith.

Such power encounters still happen today. In Southeast Asia, a young woman had been tormented for years by witchcraft. When believers prayed for her in the name of Jesus, she was delivered instantly. The transformation was so undeniable that her entire family surrendered their lives to Christ, realizing that the power of Jesus was greater than the ancestral spirits they had feared. One deliverance became the doorway to salvation for a household.

A similar breakthrough took place in the Philippines. An evangelist was opposed by a witch doctor who tried to curse his meetings. Instead of retreating, the preacher proclaimed the name of Jesus. The witch collapsed, was delivered publicly, and that same night more than three hundred villagers turned to Christ. The people could not deny what they had seen: darkness had been dethroned, and Jesus had shown Himself as Lord.

Deliverance is not a side ministry; it is frontline evangelism. Demonic powers often stand as gatekeepers over individuals, families, and communities until the power of Christ breaks in. When sorcerers boast, when curses are spoken, and when fear grips a culture, the gospel still advances through the undeniable authority of Jesus' name. These signs declare that no matter how strong the opposition may seem, the kingdom of God always prevails.

Miracles that Amplify Evangelism Efforts

Miracles do more than open individual hearts; they often cause the gospel to spread faster than any human plan could achieve. A single act of God's power can ignite revival in an entire region.

In Acts 3, Peter and John encountered a lame man at the temple gate. At the name of Jesus, the man rose and walked, leaping and praising God. The miracle drew a crowd, and Peter boldly proclaimed Christ to them. As a result, thousands believed, and the church multiplied in a single day. What began with one healing became the seed of mass evangelism.

This pattern has been repeated throughout history and continues today. In villages across Africa, Asia, and Latin

America, testimonies of miraculous healings or even resurrections have gathered entire communities to hear the gospel. One deliverance or healing spreads quickly by word of mouth, and within days or weeks, whole regions open to Christ. Human strategy may bring gradual addition, but God's power brings multiplication.

Miracles are not just events; they are catalysts. They create platforms for the gospel that no human effort could manufacture. Where one act of power reveals the compassion and authority of Jesus, many are drawn to hear and believe.

The Balance of Word and Power

Miracles are vital in evangelism and mission, but they are never meant to stand alone. Paul reminded the Corinthians that his preaching was not with persuasive words of human wisdom but in demonstration of the Spirit and of power (1 Corinthians 2:4). At the same time, he warned that faith must not rest on signs alone but on Christ Himself. The Word and the Spirit are inseparable.

A gospel of words without power is incomplete, but a gospel of power without the Word is dangerous. Miracles are signposts, not destinations. They must always point beyond themselves to the Savior. If people leave a meeting amazed by a miracle but untouched by the gospel, the mission has failed. But if the miracle softens the heart and opens the way for faith in Christ, then the Kingdom has truly advanced.

Your Role in the Great Commission

The ministry of miracles is not reserved for apostles or famous evangelists. Jesus promised that those who believe in Him will cast out demons and lay hands on the sick so that they recover (Mark 16:17–18). This promise belongs to every believer, not just a select few.

Evangelism without an expectation of God's power is only half the gospel, for the same Spirit who raised Christ from the dead lives in each of His followers.

This has been proven time and again through ordinary disciples who simply stepped out in faith. In Brazil, a group of believers who had only recently been trained in evangelism went into marketplaces to share Christ. As they prayed for the sick, reports of healing began to spread. Within weeks, entire neighborhoods were open to the gospel. It was not famous preachers who brought transformation but ordinary Christians who yielded themselves to the Spirit's power.

THOUGHTS FOR REFLECTION

1. When you think about evangelism, do you naturally expect God to confirm His Word with power? Why or why not?

2. How do miracles point people to Christ rather than distract from Him?

3. Have you ever witnessed or heard of a miracle that opened someone's heart to the gospel? How did it impact you?

4. What fears or hesitations hold you back from stepping out in faith when sharing Christ?

5. How can you rely more fully on the Holy Spirit so that your words are backed by His works?

PUT IT INTO PRACTICE

- Pray for boldness to expect God's power as you share the gospel.
- Ask the Holy Spirit to confirm your words with His works. Remember, you are not the miracle-worker; you are the vessel.

17

Living as a Vessel of God's Power

God's greatest desire has always been partnership. From Eden to the Great Commission, He chose not to bypass humanity but to work through us. Miracles are not merely heavenly interruptions. They are divine collaborations and God's limitless power flowing through yielded human vessels.

Paul described it this way: *"We have this treasure in jars of clay to show that this all-surpassing power is from God and not from us"* (2 Corinthians 4:7). In other words, the miracle-working God has chosen fragile jars of clay, ordinary men and women, to carry extraordinary glory. Miracles are not reserved for "special saints." They are God's daily intention for every believer who yields.

When Jesus declared, *"He who believes in Me... greater works than these he will do"* (John 14:12), He shattered the idea that miracles were confined to Himself alone. Every believer inherits this promise. But Christianity without demonstration is incomplete. A living faith is both confessed with our lips and confirmed through God's power at work among us.

This chapter explores what it means to live as a vessel: the posture we cultivate, the practices that keep us aligned, and the pitfalls to avoid.

The Making of a Vessel

Not every vessel carries power in the same measure. Though God can use anyone, He works most freely through those who are set apart. Availability often matters more than ability. God does not begin with a résumé but with a willing heart, like Isaiah who said, *"Here am I; send me"* (Isaiah 6:8).

Vessels are not born ready. They are shaped by God's hand. The disciples walked with Jesus for years, yet it's only after Pentecost that they became carriers of power. That kind of shaping grows through steady practices that keep us close to God.

The Word renews our minds until heaven's truth reframes how we see. *Prayer and fasting* quiet the flesh and sharpen our attention to the Spirit. *Obedience* opens the way for the supernatural, for every miracle is born of surrendered faith. A life that refuses to bend in the secret place cannot bear the weight of public demonstration.

These practices don't generate power; they prepare us to receive it. The Holy Spirit is the Miracle Worker. We do not manufacture power; we receive it as He fills us: *"You shall receive power when the Holy Spirit has come upon you"* (Acts 1:8). To be filled with the Spirit is to be enabled for His work. Miracles then move from rare exceptions to the natural overflow of a Spirit-led life. Peter's shadow healed the sick, not because shadows heal, but because the Spirit so saturated him that even his nearness carried God's power (see Acts 5:15).

Streams of Power

Scripture shows us that God's power flows through many streams, and each one reminds us that we are channels, not sources. *Prayer* makes room for God's intervention, as when Elijah prayed and fire fell from heaven (1 Kings 18:38). *Words spoken in faith* carry His authority; Jesus calmed the storm with nothing more than a command (Mark 4:39).

Compassion releases healing, since Jesus so often moved in power because He was first moved in love (Mark 1:41). *The laying on of hands* becomes a point of contact where divine power is released (Mark 16:18). *Sacrifice* clears the way for God's fire, as even a water-soaked altar burned at His response to Elijah (1 Kings 18:33–38). Even the simplest obedience unlocks the miraculous like when water turned to wine when servants filled jars at Jesus' word (John 2:7–8), and nets overflowed when Peter cast them against his logic (Luke 5:5).

The vessel never generates the power; it only carries it. A pipe does not own the river, yet the river flows through it when it stays aligned. In the same way, we do not control God's power, but when our lives are yielded, His Spirit moves like a river through us, bringing life wherever it flows.

Guarding the Vessel

Power must be guarded, because even chosen vessels can leak. Samson carried extraordinary strength yet lost it when he treated consecration lightly. *Pride* steals glory that belongs to God alone. *Unbelief* shuts down miracles before they ever take shape.

Distraction slowly suffocates intimacy and dries up the wellspring of power. The greatest threats to a miracle-shaped life are rarely external; they are the small cracks that form within. To remain usable, guard your purity, your humility, and your intimacy with God. Without them, even the strongest vessel eventually runs dry.

The purpose of power is not to magnify men but to glorify Christ. After healing the lame man at the temple gate, Peter turned the crowd's attention away from himself: *"Why do you look at us, as though by our own power or godliness we had made this man walk?"* (Acts 3:12). Every true miracle points upward, not inward. To claim glory that belongs to God is theft, but when miracles direct people to Christ, they shine as signposts of His Kingdom. And so the cry of every vessel is simple:

"Lord, make me a vessel of Your power, a channel of Your love, and a living witness of Your wonders. . Let my life be a pipeline of Your glory to my generation. Keep me pure, keep me humble, and keep me burning with Your Spirit, that through me, many may see and believe."

You were not designed to watch miracles from the sidelines but to take part in them. The God who split seas, stilled the sun, raised the dead, and healed the sick now dwells within you. You are His hands, His voice, His vessel. Your life is not ordinary. You carry within you the same Spirit who empowered Moses before Pharaoh, Elijah on Mount Carmel, Peter at Pentecost, and Paul in prison. The question is never whether God can use you but if you will let Him.

THOUGHTS FOR REFLECTION

1. In what ways have you seen yourself living as a vessel of God's power?

2. Which "cracks" (pride, distraction, unbelief, lack of consecration) do you most need to guard against right now?

3. What stream of God's power (prayer, compassion, obedience, sacrifice, etc.) is He inviting you to open more fully in your life?

4. How does knowing that the Spirit who empowered Moses, Elijah, Peter, and Paul lives in you reshape the way you view your own life?

PUT IT INTO PRACTICE

- *Expect healing:* Lay hands on the sick and pray boldly, knowing that Jesus is the same yesterday, today, and forever (Hebrews 13:8).

- *Stand in Deliverance:* Do not tolerate oppression. Declare Christ's authority over every bondage.

- *Stay yielded:* Choose obedience even when it doesn't make sense, like Peter casting the nets at Jesus' word.

- *Point upward:* When God moves through you, give the glory to Christ so that miracles serve as signposts of His Kingdom.

A Final Word

God is still performing miracles today. The Miracle-Worker continues to move in our world right now, and nothing is impossible for Him.

Though He does not need our help to perform His wonders, in His wisdom and love God often chooses to involve us. He looks for men and women who will trust Him, stand on His promises, and open their lives as vessels of His power and instruments of His purpose.

Throughout history, He has used ordinary people: Moses with a staff, Mary with a surrendered *yes*, fishermen who became apostles. None of them were perfect, yet they believed. They positioned themselves to receive and to participate in Heaven's agenda on earth.

And today, His invitation still stands. He is searching for hearts that will trust Him fully, even when the way forward is hidden in shadows. He is seeking those who will hold to His promises, even when circumstances declare the opposite. What He requires is not perfection, but a willing heart, and even faith the size of a mustard seed.

Yes, there will be challenges. Yes, there may be seasons of waiting, wrestling, and even doubting. But do not despise the days of small faith, because a spark surrendered to God can ignite a fire that hell itself cannot quench. When God finds a man or woman who dares to believe Him for the impossible, the atmosphere shifts, destinies realign, and miracles break forth.

So let me leave you with this: What are you believing in God for today? Will you lay down your fears and doubts? Will you dare to trust Him, not merely for what seems reasonable, but for what only He can do?

The Miracle-Worker is alive. His power is present. His hand is stretched forth still. And He is waiting for your yes.

Prayers for Miracles

A rchbishop Nicholas Duncan-Williams, renowned as the Apostle of Strategic Prayer, has famously said, "Prayer gives God legal authorization to intervene in the affairs of men."

If you're trusting God for a miracle, whether for yourself, your child, or someone you love, I invite you to approach these prayers with faith and expectation.

These are not prayers to rush through or recite passively. Pray them with intention. Let the words become your own as you pray, and believe that the same God who worked miracles in Scripture is still doing the impossible today.

Each prayer is grounded in the Word of God and followed by verses to declare aloud. Use these verses as declarations of faith, and stand on them until you see breakthrough. God is still watching over His Word to perform it.

PRAYERS *for* CONCEPTION

Father, I come to You in faith and through the blood of Jesus. You are the Creator and Giver of life. Thank You for making children a gift and a reward (Psalm 127:3). I align myself with Your will that Your people be fruitful and multiply (Genesis 1:28), and I stand on Your promises as I trust You for the gift of children.

Your Word says that none of Your people will be barren or miscarry (Exodus 23:26). I speak to my body and command it to come into alignment with Your Word. Just as You opened the wombs of Sarah, Rebekah, and Leah, I ask You now to open mine. Let Your healing power touch every part of my reproductive system and my partner's. Restore anything that needs to be made whole, in Jesus' name.

I declare that my body will conceive and fulfill the purpose You have for me, in the name of Jesus. Your Word promises long life and full-term pregnancies. I declare that any pregnancy You give will be carried to term—healthy, whole, and complete.

Thank You for doing wonders beyond what we can understand and miracles beyond counting (Job 5:9). Be glorified in my testimony, and let my joy be full as You fulfill the desire of my heart.

In the mighty name of Jesus, amen.

PROMISES TO DECLARE

God blessed them and said to them, 'Be fruitful and increase in
number; fill the earth and subdue it. Rule over the fish in the
sea and the birds in the sky and over every living creature that
moves on the ground.'
GENESIS 1:28

Isaac prayed to the LORD on behalf of his wife, because she
was childless. The LORD answered his prayer, and his wife
Rebekah became pregnant.
GENESIS 25:21

You must serve only the Lord your God. If you do, I will bless
you with food and water, and I will protect you from illness.
There will be no miscarriages or infertility in your land, and I
will give you long, full lives.
EXODUS 23:25-26 (NLT)

You will be blessed above all the nations of the earth. None of
your men or women will be childless, and all your livestock will
bear young.
DEUTERONOMY 7:14 (NLT)

I prayed for this child, and the LORD has granted me what I
asked of him.
1 SAMUEL 1:27

Children are a gift from the Lord;
they are a reward from him.
PSALM 127:3 (NLT)

It was by faith that even Sarah was able to have a child, though she was barren and was too old. She believed that God would keep his promise.
HEBREWS 11:11 (NLT)

He does great things too marvelous to understand. He performs countless miracles.
JOB 5:9 (NLT)

He settles the childless woman in her home as a happy mother of children. Praise the LORD.
PSALM 113:9

Your wife will be like a fruitful vine within your house; your children will be like olive shoots around your table.
PSALM 128:3

Jesus looked at them and said, 'With man this is impossible, but with God all things are possible.'
MATTHEW 19:26

PRAYERS *for*
PREGNANCY AND DELIVERY

Prayer for the Fetus

FIRST TRIMESTER

Father, every good and perfect gift comes from You (James 1:17). Thank You for the gift of new life and for the miracle taking shape in my womb. Your Word says, *"Yet you brought me out of the womb; you made me trust in you, even at my mother's breast. From birth I was cast on you; from my mother's womb you have been my God"* (Psalm 22:9–10). I thank You that this child is Yours from the very beginning.

I declare that this child is watched over, sustained, and surrounded by Your presence, in the name of Jesus. Guide every part of the development process. Let the placenta and amniotic sac form and function perfectly to support this child. I pray for balanced hormone levels and all the nutrients my body needs to nourish this pregnancy.

I speak life over every part of my baby's body. Let the brain and nervous system, the heart and blood vessels, the liver, kidneys, lungs, and all vital organs form just as You designed them. Your Word says that when You looked at what You made, You called it very good (Genesis 1:31), and I declare the same over this child.

I come against every spirit of infirmity, premature death, and complication. I declare that this child is being fearfully and wonderfully made (Psalm 139:14), protected from all harm, sickness, deformity, or disorder.

In Jesus' mighty name, amen.

SECOND TRIMESTER

Lord, I praise You for the growth and progress of this baby as they grow strong inside my womb. Thank You for the development of their organs, limbs, and senses. I stand on Your

Word in Isaiah 40:31, declaring that those who wait on You will renew their strength. I speak supernatural strength over my baby and over myself during this time.

I declare that my baby's heart, lungs, and nervous system are divinely protected as they continue to mature. This child is Your creation, and Your Word says they are fearfully and wonderfully made (Psalm 139:14).

I speak to every bone, muscle, feature, organ, and system, and I command them to align with Your Word and develop perfectly. I speak life, health, and wholeness over this child. Cover us with Your protection, fill us with Your grace, and surround us with Your favor.

In Jesus' mighty name, amen.

THIRD TRIMESTER

Thank You, Lord, for sustaining this child and me throughout this entire pregnancy. As the time of birth approaches, I ask for Your continued protection, strength, and presence during these final weeks.

I declare that my baby will develop the right amount of fat to regulate their body temperature after birth. Let their lungs fully form so they can breathe without difficulty. I speak full and healthy brain and nervous system development, and I declare that my child will have a sound and strong mind (2 Timothy 1:7).

I pray for proper positioning for a safe and smooth delivery. Let strength and immunity be transferred fully as my baby prepares to leave the womb. Strengthen them in body and spirit for the transition ahead.

I commit the entire labor and delivery process into Your hands. I come against any complications, and declare that there will be no fetal distress, no issues in the birth canal, and no entanglement with the umbilical cord. I declare that my baby's heart will remain steady and strong throughout.

I speak over my own body and declare that it will function exactly as You designed: efficiently, safely, and without unnecessary pain or intervention. Let this delivery be peaceful, smooth, and fully covered by Your presence.

In Jesus' mighty name, amen.

PROMISES TO DECLARE

God saw all that he had made, and it was very good. And there
was evening, and there was morning—the sixth day.
GENESIS 1:31

Every good and perfect gift is from above, coming down from
the Father of the heavenly lights, who does not change like
shifting shadows.
JAMES 1:17

I praise you because I am fearfully and wonderfully made; your
works are wonderful, I know that full well. **PSALM 139:14**

No one shall suffer miscarriage or be barren in your land; I will
fulfill the number of your days.
EXODUS 23:26

Yet you brought me out of the womb; you made me trust in
you, even at my mother's breast. From birth I was cast on you;
from my mother's womb you have been my God.
PSALM 22:9-10

Prayer for the Mother

Father, thank You for the precious gift of life growing inside me. I speak health and strength over my body. Let it function exactly as You designed it to. I declare that my womb is a safe and stable environment, and I cancel every attack of miscarriage or complication, in Jesus' name.

I give You my mind. Help me keep my thoughts focused on You. Your Word says You will keep in perfect peace those whose minds are stayed on You (Isaiah 26:3). Let that peace fill every part of me—spirit, soul, and body. Ease any discomfort and renew my strength each day (Isaiah 40:29–31).

As I move through this pregnancy, I declare that my body will adjust with grace. I bind fear, anxiety, and worry, and I release Your peace that surpasses all understanding (Philippians 4:7) over my heart and mind. Let Your presence be near and real to me throughout every stage.

I speak divine protection over myself and my baby. Standing on Psalm 91, I declare that no sickness, plague, or harm will come near us. Cover us, shield us, and guide us in every step (Psalm 91:10–11).

As the time of birth draws near, let strength and emotional stability be my portion. Prepare my body fully for labor and delivery. I come against every complication—preeclampsia, gestational diabetes, preterm labor, placenta previa, placental abruption, fetal distress, and anything else that would hinder a full-term, healthy birth. I declare that I will carry this baby to full term, just as You promised (Exodus 23:26).

Give wisdom to every member of my medical team. Let labor be smooth and safe, with no intervention unless truly necessary. I declare that my baby will be born healthy and strong, and that I will recover fully, without injury or delay. This pregnancy will be a testimony of Your faithfulness.

In Jesus' mighty name I pray, amen.

Promises to Declare

For he will rescue you from every trap
and protect you from deadly disease.
He will cover you with his feathers.
He will shelter you with his wings.
His faithful promises are your armor and protection.
Do not be afraid of the terrors of the night,
nor the arrow that flies in the day.
Do not dread the disease that stalks in darkness,
nor the disaster that strikes at midday.
Though a thousand fall at your side,
though ten thousand are dying around you,
these evils will not touch you.
Just open your eyes,
and see how the wicked are punished.
If you make the Lord your refuge,
if you make the Most High your shelter,
no evil will conquer you;
no plague will come near your home.
For he will order his angels
to protect you wherever you go.
They will hold you up with their hands
so you won't even hurt your foot on a stone.
Psalm 91:3-12 (NLT)

He gives power to the weak
and strength to the powerless.
Even youths will become weak and tired,
and young men will fall in exhaustion.
But those who trust in the Lord will find new strength.
They will soar high on wings like eagles.

They will run and not grow weary.
They will walk and not faint.
ISAIAH 40:29-31 (NLT)

Cast all your anxiety on him because he cares for you.
1 PETER 5:7

You will keep in perfect peace
all who trust in you,
all whose thoughts are fixed on you!
ISAIAH 26:3 (NLT)

Then you will experience God's peace, which exceeds anything
we can understand. His peace will guard your hearts and minds
as you live in Christ Jesus. PHILIPPIANS 4:7 (NLT)

I can do all this through him who gives me strength.
PHILIPPIANS 4:13

Each time he said, "My grace is all you need. My power works
best in weakness." So now I am glad to boast about my
weaknesses, so that the power of Christ can work through me.
2 CORINTHIANS 12:9 (NLT)

For I know the plans I have for you," declares the Lord, "plans
to prosper you and not to harm you, plans to give you hope
and a future.
JEREMIAH 29:11

Have I not commanded you? Be strong and courageous. Do
not be afraid; do not be discouraged, for the Lord your God
will be with you wherever you go.
JOSHUA 1:9

Because of the Lord's great love we are not consumed, for his compassions never fail.

LAMENTATIONS 3:22

Prayer for the Right Helpers and Medical Team

Father, I commit this entire journey, from pregnancy, childbirth, to postpartum care, into Your hands. From the first appointment to full recovery, go before my child and me every step of the way.

Appoint the right medical team: doctors, nurses, specialists, and midwives who are skilled, attentive, and guided by wisdom. Let their minds be sharp, their hands steady, and their decisions aligned with what is best. I pray that nothing will be missed, overlooked, or delayed.

Let communication among the medical staff be clear and timely. May I be treated with dignity, not as a number, but as a person worthy of care and respect. Meet every physical, emotional, mental, and medical need with excellence and compassion, from the first consultation to the final follow-up.

Surround me with the right support system. Send family, friends, and helpers who are present, dependable, and spiritually sensitive to my needs. Let them lift me up and strengthen me in every way. Remove any voice or influence that brings fear, stress, or discouragement.

I stand on Isaiah 52:12, and declare that You go before me and are my rear guard. I plead the blood of Jesus over every stage of this journey: prenatal care, testing, delivery, and postpartum recovery. Thank You for going ahead of me, walking beside me, and covering me from behind.

In Jesus' mighty name, amen.

PROMISES TO DECLARE

But you will not leave in haste or go in flight, for the Lord will
go before you, and the God of Israel will be your rear guard.
ISAIAH 52:12

The Lord himself goes before you and will be with you; he will
never leave you nor forsake you. Do not be afraid; do not be
discouraged.
DEUTERONOMY 31:8

You go before me and follow me.
You place your hand of blessing on my head.
PSALM 139:5 (NLT)

I will go before you and will level the mountains; I will break
down the gates of bronze and cut through the bars of iron.
ISAIAH 45:2

The Lord keeps you from all harm
and watches over your life.
The Lord keeps watch over you as you come and go,
both now and forever.
PSALM 121:7-8 (NLT)

Prayer for Babies Born Prematurely

Thank You, Lord, that my precious child is not here by accident, but by divine appointment. Though they arrived earlier than expected, I stand on the truth that nothing catches You by surprise. You are Jehovah Rapha, my Healer (Exodus 15:26), and Jehovah Jireh, my Provider (Genesis 22:14).

I declare that my child will live, grow strong, and fulfill every purpose You have for them (Jeremiah 29:11). Every organ, every system, and every stage of development is under Your care. I place my child in Your hands, and I choose to trust not in what I see, but in who You are—the Creator, the Sustainer, and the One who always finishes what He starts (Philippians 1:6).

IMMUNE SYSTEM (PROTECTION AGAINST INFECTIONS)

Lord, I ask You to strengthen my baby's immune system with supernatural power. Let every cell work in perfect order, ready to resist and overcome infections, illnesses, and complications.

I stand on Your promise in Psalm 91:10: "No harm will overtake you; no disaster will come near your tent." I declare that my child is covered and protected under the shadow of the Almighty (Psalm 91:1). Let their body grow strong, their immune system be empowered, and their health be preserved by Your hand. No virus, no bacteria, no infection shall prosper against them.

In Jesus' name, amen.

RESPIRATORY SYSTEM

In the name of Jesus, I speak life and strength over my baby's lungs. I declare that every part of their respiratory system will develop fully and function exactly as You designed. Let every breath be steady, strong, and unhindered.

I stand on Ezekiel 37:5: *"I will make breath enter you, and you will come to life.*" Let this Word come alive in my baby. I rebuke every form of respiratory distress, underdevelopment, or damage, and I call forth complete healing. My child will breathe freely, live fully, and testify of Your power.

In Jesus' name. Amen.

NERVOUS SYSTEM

Lord, I lift up my baby's brain and nervous system to You. I declare full healing and development in every area. In the name of Jesus, I cancel every assignment of neurological disorder, delay, or dysfunction. Let every neural connection, reflex, and response form perfectly.

I declare intelligence, alertness, and mental capacity beyond expectation. According to Jeremiah 29:11, You have plans for my child, plans to prosper and not to harm, plans to give a future filled with hope. I declare their brain function will be flawless, their coordination will be strong, and they will thrive in every area of life, to the glory of God.

In Jesus' name, amen.

DIGESTIVE SYSTEM AND NUTRITION

Father, I lift up my baby's digestive system before You. I speak healing and order over every part of their body responsible for nourishment and growth. Let their system absorb nutrients efficiently and function without complication.

I declare that every feeding will be successful. My child will gain weight consistently and thrive. Reverse any issues related to digestion or feeding. This baby will eat, grow, and develop just as You ordained. They will be strong, healthy, and full of life.

In Jesus' name, amen.

GENERAL GROWTH AND REVERSING PERMANENT DAMAGE

Lord, let every organ, muscle, and tissue in my baby grow

according to Your perfect plan. I declare that my child will meet all developmental milestones on time, from sitting and walking to speaking and learning. Your Word says, *"I praise You because I am fearfully and wonderfully made"* (Psalm 139:14). Let this truth be visible in every part of their growth.

In the name of Jesus, I ask You to reverse every effect of premature birth. Let Your healing power flow through my child from head to toe. I declare no lasting damage, no learning disabilities, no physical limitations, and no developmental delays. What was meant for harm, You are turning for good (Genesis 50:20). I speak wholeness, excellence, and purpose over their life.

In Jesus' name, amen.

RELEASE FROM NICU AND FUTURE HEALTH

Father, I pray for a smooth recovery and a swift release from the NICU in perfect health. Give the doctors and nurses wisdom and precision as they care for my child. I declare Isaiah 53:5: *"By His wounds, we are healed."* Heal every part of my baby's body and let them thrive without setbacks.

I declare that my child is blessed and highly favored (Luke 1:28). They will grow up strong, smart, and healthy. There will be no complications and no long-term issues; they will live a life full of joy and purpose. I trust You completely and thank You in advance for their healing.

In Jesus' name, amen.

Promises to Declare

Every good and perfect gift is from above, coming down from the Father of the heavenly lights, who does not change like shifting shadows.
James 1:17

No harm will overtake you, no disaster will come near your tent.
Psalm 91:10

I will make breath enter you, and you will come to life.
Ezekiel 37:5

Don't be afraid, for I am with you.
Don't be discouraged, for I am your God.
I will strengthen you and help you.
I will hold you up with my victorious right hand.
Isaiah 41:10 (NLT)

For I know the plans I have for you," declares the Lord, "plans to prosper you and not to harm you, plans to give you hope and a future.
Jeremiah 29:11

I praise you because I am fearfully and wonderfully made; your works are wonderful, I know that full well.
Psalm 139:14

But he was pierced for our transgressions, he was crushed for our iniquities; the punishment that brought us peace was on him, and by his wounds we are healed.
Isaiah 53:5

O Lord, you alone are my hope.
I've trusted you, O Lord, from childhood.
⁶ Yes, you have been with me from birth;
from my mother's womb you have cared for me.
No wonder I am always praising you!
PSALM 71:5-6 (NLT)

I will be your God throughout your lifetime—
until your hair is white with age.
I made you, and I will care for you.
I will carry you along and save you.
ISAIAH 46:4 (NLT)

Let us, your servants, see you work again;
let our children see your glory.
PSALM 90:16 (NLT)

Now all glory to God, who is able, through his mighty power at
work within us, to accomplish infinitely more than we might
ask or think.
EPHESIANS 3:20 (NLT)

Cast all your anxiety on him because he cares for you.
1 PETER 5:7

I knew you before I formed you in your mother's womb.
Before you were born I set you apart
and appointed you as my prophet to the nations.
JEREMIAH 1:5 (NLT)

Since he did not spare even his own Son but gave him up for us
all, won't he also give us everything else?
ROMANS 8:32 (NLT)

And I am certain that God, who began the good work within you, will continue his work until it is finally finished on the day when Christ Jesus returns.

PHILIPPIANS 1:6 (NLT)

Prayer to Dedicate the Child(ren) to God

When Jesus was born, He was dedicated in the temple (Luke 2:22–35). During that moment of dedication, prophetic words were spoken over Him by Simeon and Anna; those words confirmed His identity and purpose. In the same way, what we speak over our children carries great power. Our words shape their future.

Declare this prayer with faith, inserting your child's name wherever [child's name] appears:

[Child's name] will be great in the land. They will rise and thrive. They will fulfill God's assignment for their life and walk boldly in the path He has prepared. They will be blessed with wisdom, strength, and honor. They will live in good health, with a sound mind. No harm will come near them, and the blessing of the Lord will rest upon their life (Psalm 91:10, Proverbs 10 22). I declare that with long life, the Lord will satisfy [child's name] and show them His salvation (Psalm 91:16).

I also pray that **[parents' or caretakers' names]** will be provided for—spiritually, financially, and emotionally—so that we may raise [child's name] with excellence and care. Every need will be met by God's supply. I release wisdom, knowledge, understanding, favor, grace, and the blessing that adds no sorrow over [child's name].

[Child's name] will increase in wisdom, stature, and favor with God and with people (Luke 2:52). Their life, calling, and destiny are secured in Christ. No weapon formed against them will prosper (Isaiah 54:17), and anything not planted by God in their life will be uprooted (Matthew 15:13).

They will be preserved from sickness, harm, danger, and anything that hinders their purpose. [Child's name] will grow strong—in body, mind, and spirit. They will be powerful in their generation, a light in dark places, and a world-changer for the glory of God.

None of their blessings will be stolen. They will not labor in vain or build what others take away (Isaiah 65:21–23). They will hear God clearly, know His voice, and follow His will. The Spirit of God will guide them, and their purpose will not be delayed or sabotaged. As their days, so shall their strength be (Deuteronomy 33:25).

The Lord will be their Defender, their Rock, and the stronghold of their life (Psalm 18:2).

In Jesus' name, amen.

PROMISES TO DECLARE

Here am I and the children whom the Lord has given me! We
are for signs and wonders in Israel From the Lord of hosts,
Who dwells in Mount Zion.
ISAIAH 8:18

'And I myself will be a wall of fire around it,' declares the Lord,
'and I will be its glory within.'
ZECHARIAH 2:5

May the bolts of your gates be of iron and bronze;
may you be secure all your days.
DEUTERONOMY 33:25 (NLT)

Jesus grew in wisdom and in stature and in favor with God and
all the people.
LUKE 2:52 (NLT)

If you, then, though you are evil, know how to give good gifts
to your children, how much more will your Father in heaven
give good gifts to those who ask him!
MATTHEW 7:11

The Lord is my rock, my fortress, and my savior;
my God is my rock, in whom I find protection.
He is my shield, the power that saves me,
and my place of safety.
PSALM 18:2 (NLT)

Their children will be successful everywhere;
an entire generation of godly people will be blessed.
PSALM 112:2 (NLT)

But the Lord says,
"The captives of warriors will be released,
and the plunder of tyrants will be retrieved.
For I will fight those who fight you,
and I will save your children.
ISAIAH 49:25 (NLT)

All your children will be taught by the Lord, and great will be
their peace.
ISAIAH 54:13

Once I was young, and now I am old.
Yet I have never seen the godly abandoned
or their children begging for bread.
PSALM 37:25 (NLT)

But in that coming day
no weapon turned against you will succeed.
You will silence every voice
raised up to accuse you.
These benefits are enjoyed by the servants of the Lord;
their vindication will come from me.
I, the Lord, have spoken!
ISAIAH 54:17 (NLT)

PRAYERS *for*
HEALING MIRACLES

Father, You are the God who heals and restores. When doctors run out of answers, You still have the final Word. Today, I bring this sickness before You and declare that by the stripes of Jesus, healing has already been provided. I reject every report of death, decline, or defeat, and I speak life and restoration over this body. Let Your healing power flow from the crown of the head to the soles of the feet.

Lord, I thank You not only for healing but also for the promise of divine health. I ask that every system, organ, and cell in this body come into alignment with Your Word. Let strength, vitality, and wholeness be my portion.

Teach me to walk daily in wisdom, so that I may guard the health You have given me. May my life testify that You are the Lord who heals and the God who sustains.

I believe that nothing is too hard for You, and I trust You to turn this impossible situation into a testimony of Your glory.

In Jesus' name, amen.

PROMISES TO DECLARE

By His stripes we are healed.
ISAIAH 53:5 (NKJV)

But I will restore you to health and heal your wounds, declares
the Lord
JEREMIAH 30:17

Praise the Lord, my soul… who forgives all your sins and heals
all your diseases.
PSALM 103:2–3

For I am the Lord, who heals you.
EXODUS 15:26

Beloved, I pray that you may prosper in all things and be in
health, just as your soul prospers.
3 JOHN 1:2 (NKJV)

Worship the Lord your God, and his blessing will be on your
food and water. I will take away sickness from among you.
EXODUS 23:25

But those who hope in the Lord will renew their strength. They
will soar on wings like eagles; they will run and not grow weary,
they will walk and not be faint.
ISAIAH 40:31

PRAYERS *for*
PROVISION MIRACLES

Heavenly Father, You are Jehovah Jireh, the God who provides. I bring every financial need and every place of lack before You today. Where doors have been shut, I ask You to open new ones. Where resources have been scarce, I declare overflow. Let unexpected provision, divine opportunities, and supernatural favor locate me and my family.

But Lord, I thank You not only for meeting urgent needs, but for Your promise of abundant living. Teach me to walk in stewardship, wisdom, and generosity so that lack will not return. Let my life be a testimony that Your blessing makes rich and adds no sorrow with it. Fill my hands with resources, my mind with creative ideas, and my heart with contentment. I declare that I will not just survive but thrive, because my supply comes from You.

I trust You to turn insufficiency into abundance and scarcity into overflow.

In Jesus' name, amen.

PROMISES TO DECLARE

And my God will meet all your needs according to the riches of
his glory in Christ Jesus.
PHILIPPIANS 4:19

And God is able to bless you abundantly, so that in all things at
all times, having all that you need, you will abound in every
good work.
2 CORINTHIANS 9:8

The Lord will grant you abundant prosperity... The Lord will
open the heavens, the storehouse of his bounty, to send rain on
your land in season and to bless all the work of your hands.
DEUTERONOMY 28:11–12

I have come that they may have life, and have it to the full.
JOHN 10:10

The Lord is my shepherd, I lack nothing.
PSALM 23:1

The Bring the whole tithe into the storehouse, that there may
be food in my house. Test me in this," says the LORD
Almighty, "and see if I will not throw open the floodgates of
heaven and pour out so much blessing that there will not be
room enough to store it.
MALACHI 3:10

The Lord is my shepherd, I lack nothing.
PSALM 23:1

PRAYERS *for*
RESTORATION
MIRACLES

Lord, You are the God who makes all things new. I bring before You every area of my life that feels broken, wasted, or stolen. Where years have been lost, restore them. Where relationships have been shattered, mend them. Where opportunities have slipped away, redeem them.

Lord, I thank You that Your restoration is greater than what was lost. I declare that the enemy must release everything he has stolen, and that You are turning mourning into dancing and ashes into beauty. I trust You to breathe new life where there has been barrenness, peace where there has been strife, and hope where there has been despair.

Teach me to walk in wholeness, forgiveness, and renewed purpose. Let my life declare that nothing is beyond Your reach, and that what You restore comes back multiplied and better than before.

In Jesus' name, amen.

PROMISES TO DECLARE

I will repay you for the years the locusts have eaten… You will have plenty to eat, until you are full, and you will praise the name of the Lord your God.
JOEL 2:25–26

But I will restore you to health and heal your wounds, declares the Lord.
JEREMIAH 30:17

I will bring my people Israel back from exile. They will rebuild the ruined cities and live in them. They will plant vineyards and drink their wine; they will make gardens and eat their fruit.
AMOS 9:14

Instead of your shame you will receive a double portion… and everlasting joy will be yours.
ISAIAH 61:7

But I will restore you to health and heal your wounds, declares the Lord.
JEREMIAH 30:17

After Job had prayed for his friends, the Lord restored his fortunes and gave him twice as much as he had before
JOB 42:10

Let us then approach God's throne of grace with confidence, so that we may receive mercy and find grace to help us in our time of need.
HEBREWS 4:16

Notes

Introduction
Elwell, W. A. (Ed.). (1996). Evangelical dictionary of theology (p. 778).
Baker Books.

Chapter 1
Elwell, W. A. (Ed.). (1996). Evangelical dictionary of theology (p. 778).
Baker Books.
Scroggie, W. G. (1995). A guide to the Gospels. Pickering & Inglis.
Lewis,   C.   S.   (2015).   Miracles.   HarperOne.

Chapter 2
Elwell, W. A. (Ed.). (1996). Evangelical dictionary of theology (p. 779).
Baker Books.

About the Author

D r. Kibby Otoo is an established life coach, mentor, and pastor who has traveled extensively, impacting lives, organizations, and communities around the world. A graduate of Oral Roberts University, he is a charismatic leader, engaging speaker, prolific writer, and overseer of churches throughout North America.

He has served with distinction in various ministerial roles. Most notably, he was the National Coordinator for Global Strategic Prayer, where he worked with intercessors worldwide to equip believers to thrive in the face of life's challenges.

Through his non-profit organization, Transcontinental Empowerment Corporation (TEC), Dr. Kibby continues to bring hope and healing to individuals, families, and communities. He also serves on the advisory panel of Gateway2Missions, an international aid organization dedicated to ending extreme poverty in parts of Africa.

As a trusted life coach and mentor, he has guided numerous business owners and professionals in navigating the complex challenges of living out their calling.

To learn more about Dr. Kibby Otoo, follow him on Facebook and Instagram (@drkibbyotoo), or visit www.drkibbyotoo.net.

www.ingramcontent.com/pod-product-compliance
Lightning Source LLC
Chambersburg PA
CBHW070820120626
46556CB00002B/596